THE CORTEZ PETERS CHAMPIONSHIP TYPING DRILLS

AN INDIVIDUALIZED DIAGNOSTIC/ PRESCRIPTIVE METHOD FOR DEVELOPING ACCURACY AND SPEED

Second Edition

CORTEZ PETERS
Undefeated Champion Typist

GREGG DIVISION/McGRAW-HILL BOOK COMPANY

New York Atlanta Dallas St. Louis San Francisco Auckland Bogotá
Guatemala Hamburg Lisbon London Madrid Mexico Milan Montreal
New Delhi Panama Paris San Juan São Paulo Singapore Sydney
Tokyo Toronto

Sponsoring Editors: Gina M. Ferrara, Barbara N. Oakley
Editing Supervisor: Elizabeth Huffman
Design and Art Supervisor: Nancy Axelrod
Production Supervisor: Priscilla Taguer

Cover Designer: Karen Tureck
Photographer: Ken Karp

CREDITS

Accuracy Study 26, pages 80–81: Drills 1 through 7 are adapted from
Guyton, Arthur C.: *Textbook of Medical Physiology,* ©1976 by the W. B. Saunders
Company, Philadelphia, Pennsylvania.

Accuracy Study 29, pages 85–88: The practice materials in Drills 1 through 5
and 7 through 15 are based on items that appeared in the "Gobbledygook"
column of *The Washington Star* and are reproduced here by permission of
The Star.

Library of Congress Cataloging-in-Publication Data

Peters, Cortez.
  THE CORTEZ PETERS CHAMPIONSHIP TYPING DRILLS.

  1. Typewriting. I. Title. II. Title: Championship
typing drills.
Z49.P479 1987   642.3   86-21428
ISBN 0-07-049637-4

THE CORTEZ PETERS CHAMPIONSHIP TYPING DRILLS, Second Edition

  34567890 WEBWEB 8943210987

ISBN 0-07-049637-4

▨▨▨▨▨▨▨
CONTENTS

To the User		iv
Section 1	Diagnostic Charts	1
	Speed and Accuracy Chart	2
	Skill-Development Paragraph Record	2
	Sample Exercises 1 and 2	3
	Error-Analysis Chart	4
	Speed and Accuracy Analysis	6
	Sample Exercise 3	8
	Answer Key	12
Section 2	Championship Warmup Drills	13
Section 3	5-Minute Timings	15
Section 4	Diagnostic Tests	31
Section 5	Skill-Development Paragraphs	34
Section 6	Accuracy Studies	41
	1 Simple-Vocabulary Words	42
	2 High-Stroke-Intensity Words	43
	3 Alternate-Hand Words	45
	4 Compound- and Multiple-Stroke Words	46
	5 Vertical-Stroke Words	47
	6 Double-Letter Words	50
	7 One-Hand Words	51
	8 Alphabetic Words	52
	9 Spacing Drill	57
	10 Shifting Drill	58
	11 Left Hand, First Finger	59
	12 Right Hand, First Finger	61
	13 Left Hand, Second Finger	62
	14 Right Hand, Second Finger	63
	15 Left Hand, Third Finger	64
	16 Right Hand, Third Finger	65

Section 6 (Cont.)	17 Left Hand, Fourth Finger	65
	18 Right Hand, Fourth Finger	66
	19 Left-Hand Words	67
	20 Right-Hand Words	68
	21 Punctuation	69
	22 Concentration Drills—Similar Words	70
	23 Concentration Drills—Long Words	73
	24 Concentration Drills—Unusual Words	75
	25 Intensive Concentration Drills—Paragraphs	77
	26 Intensive Concentration Drills—Paragraphs/Unusual Words	79
	27 Intensive Concentration Drills—Reverse Typing	81
	28 Concentration Drills—Split Doublets	84
	29 Concentration Drills—Paragraphs	85
Section 7	Speed Studies	89
	1 Simple-Vocabulary Sentences	90
	2 High-Stroke-Intensity Sentences	92
	3 Alternate-Hand Sentences	94
	4 Compound- and Multiple-Stroke Sentences	96
	5 Vertical-Stroke Sentences	97
	6 Double-Letter Sentences	98
	7 One-Hand-Word Sentences	100
	8 Alphabetic Sentences	101
	9 Frequent-Spacing Sentences	103
	10 Frequent-Shifting Sentences	104

TO THE USER

The Cortez Peters Championship Typing Drills represents a proven concept in developing speed and accuracy at the typewriter. Two distinguishing features of this book are its diagnostic approach and its utilization of championship typing drills.

It is the continuity of the drills practiced in uninterrupted blocks of time that provides the best results. Maximum benefit will be derived by devoting a five- or six-week block of time each semester or quarter to the drills in this book, with Monday and Friday serving as the Pretest and Posttest days and Tuesday, Wednesday, and Thursday serving as the corrective practice days. Consequently, students develop superior keyboarding skills and need less time for production typing assignments.

During the first semester or quarter of the Cortez Peters Championship Typing System, the emphasis is on accuracy development—reducing the class error rate to 3 or less on 5-minute timings. Thereafter, the emphasis is on developing speed, yet maintaining a high degree of accuracy.

Provided in this second edition is an Agenda of Class Activities outlining how to use these materials on a daily basis. Detailed instruction is also provided on how to complete the charts. Along with some minor editing changes, additional drill material has been added. For the convenience of the user, the sequence of the drill material has been reorganized so that it appears in the sequence in which it is used.

Additional methods, strategies, diagnostic aids, and teaching aids are available from the author.

INTRODUCTION

This book is divided into seven sections. The sections are as follows: (1) Diagnostic Charts, (2) Championship Warmup Drills, (3) 5-Minute Timings, (4) Diagnostic Tests, (5) Skill-Development Paragraphs, (6) Accuracy Studies, and (7) Speed Studies.

1. Diagnostic Charts. The diagnostic charts enable the user to record and analyze his or her typing performance, thereby identifying areas of weakness. There are three diagnostic charts in all—Chart 1: Speed and Accuracy Chart, Chart 2: Error-Analysis Chart, and Chart 3: Speed and Accuracy Analysis. The success of the program hinges on the accurate use of the diagnostic charts. Therefore, the user should review the charts three to five days prior to the beginning of the program. The complete explanation of how to utilize each chart is explained in detail in Section 1. Sample exercises are also provided for the three charts.

2. Championship Warmup Drills. These warmup drills, which contain basic stroke combinations, should be done on a daily basis.

3. 5-Minute Timings. There are fifteen 5-minute timings. Five of these timings are used as Pretests. The rest are used to measure progress. Errors are analyzed on the top half of Chart 2: Error-Analysis Chart. The bottom half of this chart directs the user to the appropriate drills to remedy the weaknesses that were identified in the Pretest.

4. Diagnostic Tests. The diagnostic tests consist of ten 1-minute timings on specially constructed sentences, each of which stresses a particular reach or stroke combination. Results are recorded on Chart 3: Speed and Accuracy Analysis. Corrective practice is assigned according to individual needs.

5. Skill-Development Paragraphs. These 1-minute speed paragraphs range in length from 20 to 130 words a minute (WAM). The user strives to complete each paragraph without error in 1 minute. Five 1-minute timings should be taken during the last 10 minutes of each day during the corrective practice sessions.

6. Accuracy Studies. There are twenty-nine accuracy studies in all, with each accuracy study containing several groups of drill lines. The types of errors that are made on the Pretest determine which accuracy studies will be practiced.

7. Speed Studies. There are ten speed studies, with each speed study containing several groups of drill lines. Every speed study stresses different speed stroke combinations. The amount of errors that are made on the Pretest determines whether or not accuracy and/or speed studies will be practiced.

Although the accuracy and speed studies are both considered corrective practice, accuracy studies should always be practiced before speed studies.

HOW TO USE THIS PROGRAM

As recommended earlier, maximum benefit will be derived by devoting a five- or six-week block of time each semester or quarter to this program. In order to use all the materials in this book effectively, the Agenda of Class Activities on page vi indicates which materials should be used during each weekly sequence. Some users may need additional time to chart their errors during the first week. If so, you could add up to a week using the following schedule:

DAY 1
Two 5-minute timings on Timed Writing 1, p. 16. Compute GWAM and NWAM; post to Chart 1.

DAY 2
Classify and record errors, prioritize corrective practice, and fill out Chart 2.

DAY 3
Ten 1-minute timings on Diagnostic Test 1, p. 32. Compute CWAM.

DAY 4
Fill out Chart 3 and prioritize the corrective practice.

DAY 5
Review the charting and arithmetic computations.

In addition, you would have to make the following changes in the Week 1 agenda:

DAY 1
Corrective practice

Five 1-minute timings
Skill-Development Paragraphs, pp. 35–40

Note: If you are using *The Cortez Peters Championship Typing Rhythm-Development Tapes*, the tapes are to be used for the entire fourth week. In that event, the fourth-week activities are to be conducted during the fifth week, while the fifth-week activities are to be conducted during the sixth week. These tapes are available directly from the author.

In summary, each weekly learning sequence will consist of the following five activities: Pretest, DIAGNOSIS, Practice, Posttest, and APPRAISAL—with emphasis on the diagnosis and appraisal. These are the key activities in the Agenda of Class Activities.

As you can see, *The Cortez Peters Championship Typing Drills* constitutes a complete speed-building and accuracy-development typing program. The diagnostic tests enable students to identify their speed and accuracy problems, and the drills enable students to correct them.

ACKNOWLEDGMENT

The author wishes to express his appreciation to Mrs. Mary Balmer for her invaluable assistance in developing and testing some of the materials in the book.

Cortez Peters

AGENDA OF CLASS ACTIVITIES

WEEK 1	WEEK 2	WEEK 3	WEEK 4	WEEK 5
DAY 1: PRETEST/DIAGNOSIS Two 5-minute timings Timed Writing 1, p. 16 Ten 1-minute timings Diagnostic Test 1, p. 32 Complete Charts 1, 2, and 3	**DAY 1: PRETEST/DIAGNOSIS** Two 5-minute timings Timed Writing 3, p. 18 Ten 1-minute timings Diagnostic Test 2, p. 32 Complete Charts 1, 2, and 3	**DAY 1: PRETEST/DIAGNOSIS** Two 5-minute timings Timed Writing 5, p. 20 Ten 1-minute timings Diagnostic Test 3, p. 32 Complete Charts 1, 2, and 3	**DAY 1: PRETEST/DIAGNOSIS** Two 5-minute timings Timed Writing 8, p. 23 Ten 1-minute timings Diagnostic Test 4, p. 33 Complete Charts 1, 2, and 3	**DAY 1: PRETEST/DIAGNOSIS** Two 5-minute timings Timed Writing 11, p. 26 Ten 1-minute timings Diagnostic Test 5, p. 33 Complete Charts 1, 2, and 3
DAY 2: PRACTICE Corrective practice* Five 1-minute timings Skill-Development Paragraphs, pp. 35–40	**DAY 2: PRACTICE** Corrective practice* Five 1-minute timings Skill-Development Paragraphs, pp. 35–40	**DAY 2: PRACTICE** Corrective practice* Five 1-minute timings Skill-Development Paragraphs, pp. 35–40	**DAY 2: PRACTICE** Corrective practice* Five 1-minute timings Skill-Development Paragraphs, pp. 35–40	**DAY 2: PRACTICE** Corrective practice* Five 1-minute timings Skill-Development Paragraphs, pp. 35–40
DAY 3: PRACTICE Corrective practice* Five 1-minute timings Skill-Development Paragraphs, pp. 35–40	**DAY 3: PRACTICE** Corrective practice* Five 1-minute timings Skill-Development Paragraphs, pp. 35–40	**DAY 3: PRACTICE** Two 5-minute timings Timed Writing 6, p. 21 Five 1-minute timings Skill-Development Paragraphs, pp. 35–40 Complete Charts 1 and 2	**DAY 3: PRACTICE** Two 5-minute timings Timed Writing 9, p. 24 Five 1-minute timings Skill-Development Paragraphs, pp. 35–40 Complete Charts 1 and 2	**DAY 3: PRACTICE** Corrective practice* Five 1-minute timings Skill-Development Paragraphs, pp. 35–40
DAY 4: PRACTICE Corrective practice* Five 1-minute timings Skill-Development Paragraphs, pp. 35–40	**DAY 4: PRACTICE** Corrective practice* Five 1-minute timings Skill-Development Paragraphs, pp. 35–40	**DAY 4: PRACTICE** Corrective practice* Five 1-minute timings Skill-Development Paragraphs, pp. 35–40	**DAY 4: PRACTICE** Corrective practice* Five 1-minute timings Skill-Development Paragraphs, pp. 35–40	**DAY 4: PRACTICE** Two 5-minute timings Timed Writing 12, p. 27 Two 5-minute timings Timed Writing 13, p. 28 Five 1-minute timings Skill-Development Paragraphs, pp. 35–40 Complete Charts 1 and 2
DAY 5: POSTTEST/APPRAISAL Two 5-minute timings Timed Writing 2, p. 17 Ten 1-minute timings Diagnostic Test 1, p. 32 Complete Charts 1, 2, and 3	**DAY 5: POSTTEST/APPRAISAL** Two 5-minute timings Timed Writing 4, p. 19 Ten 1-minute timings Diagnostic Test 2, p. 32 Complete Charts 1, 2, and 3	**DAY 5: POSTTEST/APPRAISAL** Two 5-minute timings Timed Writing 7, p. 22 Ten 1-minute timings Diagnostic Test 3, p. 32 Complete Charts 1, 2, and 3	**DAY 5: POSTTEST/APPRAISAL** Two 5-minute timings Timed Writing 10, p. 25 Ten 1-minute timings Diagnostic Test 4, p. 33 Complete Charts 1, 2, and 3	**DAY 5: POSTTEST/APPRAISAL** Two 5-minute timings Timed Writing 14, p. 29 Two 5-minute timings Timed Writing 15, p. 30 Ten 1-minute timings Diagnostic Test 5, p. 33 Complete Charts 1, 2, and 3

*When doing corrective practice, all accuracy studies (Charts 2 and 3) should be completed before going on to the speed studies (Chart 3).

SECTION 1

DIAGNOSTIC CHARTS

The diagnostic charts on pages 9–11 enable the user to record and analyze his or her typing performance, thereby identifying areas of weakness. The accurate use of these charts is *essential* to the success of the program. Section 1 explains in detail how to complete (fill in) the charts. Since they are explained in such detail, sample exercises, along with the answer key, have been provided on pages 3, 8, and 12. These exercises will allow you to apply the concepts you have just read. It is suggested that you review the charts three to five days prior to the beginning of the program.

CHART 1A
SPEED AND ACCURACY CHART

The Speed and Accuracy Chart on page 9 provides you with a clear picture of how you are progressing in your speed and accuracy studies. You will record on Chart 1A your speed scores for all 5-minute timings. You will record your gross words a minute (GWAM), that is, total words typed divided by 5 (rounded off). You will also record your net words a minute (NWAM), that is, gross words minus a 2-word penalty for each error. For example, for Timed Writing 9, assume you typed 188 words in 5 minutes and made 6 errors. Your GWAM speed would be 188 ÷ 5 = 38 and your NWAM speed would be 38 words a minute minus 12 (6 × 2) or 26 NWAM. Beginning with Timed Writing 1, you should try to improve your net words a minute speed on all 5-minute timings.

Steps in Completing Chart 1A

1. On the bottom line of the chart, in the box labeled "Date," indicate the month by writing the figure in the upper half of the box and indicate the day by writing the figure in the lower half of the box.

2. On the preceding line of the chart, in the box labeled "Errors," write the total number of errors made on the 5-minute timing. Record the better of the two timings.

Example: Assuming you made 6 errors on Timed Writing 9, you would write the number 6 in the Errors box of Column 9. (See Sample Chart 1A above.)

3. At the left and right of the chart are numbers going from 0 to 120. These numbers represent speed in words a minute (WAM). Place a dot, in the center of the column, on the line corresponding to your GWAM speed score and place another dot on the line corresponding to your NWAM speed score.

Example: Assuming that your GWAM on Timed Writing 9 was 38 and your NWAM was 26, you would place a dot on line 38 and another on line 26 in Column 9.

4. Connect the top dot you just made to the previous top dot with a straight line. Likewise, connect the bottom dot to the previous bottom dot. If you make no errors on a timing, use only one dot to reflect both GWAM and NWAM. (See Timed Writing 8 in Sample Chart 1A for a timing with no errors.)

EXERCISE: Review the sample of Timed Writing 1 on page 3. Determine your GWAM and NWAM. Complete the sample of Chart 1A below the timing based on the results. Check your work with the key on page 12.

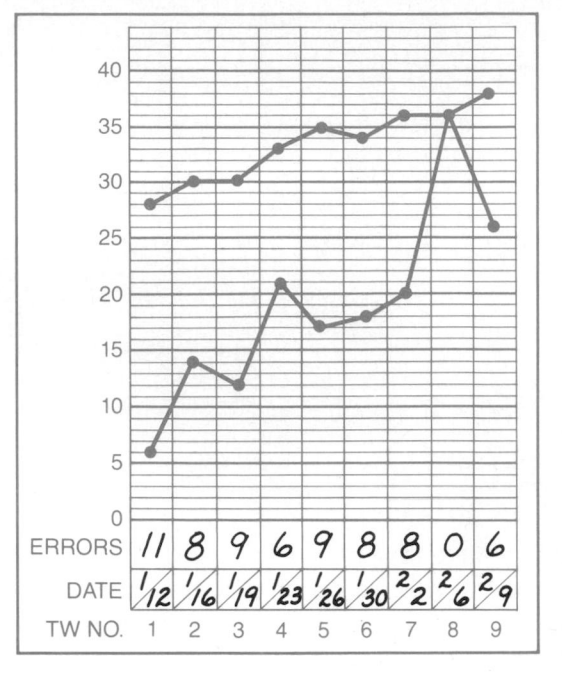

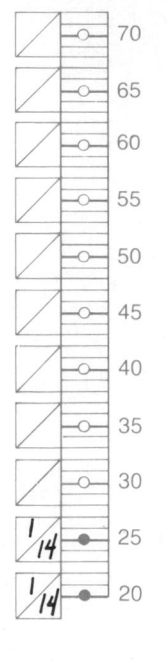

SAMPLE CHART 1A

CHART 1B

CHART 1B
SKILL-DEVELOPMENT PARAGRAPH RECORD

Beginning with the 20 WAM paragraph, you will take five 1-minute timings on all corrective practice days. As soon as you have typed the 20 WAM paragraph without error, go on to the 25 WAM paragraph. You will progress to the next paragraph every time you complete the preceding one with 100 percent accuracy.

Steps in Completing Chart 1B

1. On the first try, assume that you completed the 20 WAM paragraph with no errors. Therefore, you will record the date and fill in the white circle at 20 on the vertical bar of Chart 1B.

2. You are now on the 25 WAM paragraph. Assume that after the third try (fourth 1-minute timing) you complete the 25 WAM paragraph with no errors. You will fill in the white circle at 25 WAM.

3. On your fifth timing (first one at 30 WAM), assume you are unable to complete the 30 WAM paragraph. The 30 WAM circle cannot be filled in. You will continue with the 30 WAM paragraph the next time you do this exercise.

SAMPLE EXERCISES 1 AND 2

Timed Writing 1 (Part 1 of the Pretest)

	Words
During more than a quarter of a century, about ten thousand people	13
have learned the art of typewriting under my direct instruction. During	28
this period of time. there has not been one person who did not (acheive) this	43
facility, and this includes people from practically every background.	57
However, during my (fijth) year as an instructor, a young woman from	71
(NOrth) Carolina entered our college. Her name was Ruth. She had been the	86
valedictorian of her high school class, and (shealso) maintained an excel-	100
lent academic average (our at) school, except in the subject (ot) typewriting.	115
It was my unfortunate duty to have to deny her a place on the honor roll	130
during her (forst) year. She had the worst finger (corrdination) imagin	145

| 1 | 2 | 3 | 4 | 5 | 6 | 7 | 8 | 9 | 10 | 11 | 12 | 13 | 14 | 15 |

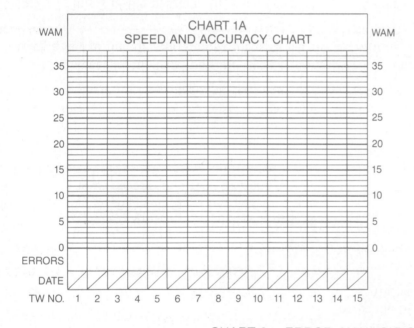

CHART 1A
SPEED AND ACCURACY CHART

CHART 2   ERROR-ANALYSIS CHART

Sequence of Corrective Practice Drills

1. Concentration
2. Letters of the Alphabet
3. Punctuation, Shifting, and Spacing
4. Fingers
5. Hands
6. Total Errors

TW NO.	LEFT-HAND ERROR SUMMARY FINGER					LEFT-HAND KEYS																RIGHT-HAND KEYS										RIGHT-HAND ERROR SUMMARY FINGER					Punctuation Errors	Shifting Errors	Spacing Errors	Concentration Errors	Total Errors
	4th	3d	2d	1st	Tot.Lt.	Q	A	Z	W	S	X	E	D	C	R	F	V	T	G	B	Y	H	N	U	J	M	I	K	O	L	P	1st	2d	3d	4th	Tot.Rt.					
1																																									

Max. Errors Allowed	1	2	2	3	4	1	1	1	1	1	1	1	1	1	1	1	1	1	1	1	1	1	1	1	1	1	1	1	1	1	1	3	2	2	1	4	1	1	1	2	5
Accuracy Study	17	15	13	11	19	17	1	26	23	19	24	5	4	3	18	6	22	20	7	2	25	8	14	21	10	13	9	11	15	12	16	12	14	16	18	20	21	10	9		7
Pages	65-66	64	62-63	59-60	67-68	55	52	57	56	55	56	53	53	53	55	53	56	56	53	53	56	54	55	56	54	54	54	54	55	54	55	61-62	63-64	65	66	68	69-70	58-59	57-58	*	51-52
PL	3	3	3	3	5	5	5	5	5	5	5	5	5	5	5	5	5	5	5	5	5	5	5	5	5	5	5	5	5	5	5	3	3	3	3	5	3	3	10		3
Wk 1																																									

ACCURACY STUDY 8/Drill No.

1 (typing) (i) one of (the) most important (waysof) conveying (informatiun)

2 (YOu), the typist, (will) be (judfed) by (teh) quality of (yhe) product (poduced;)

3 and (yout) attitude will be (dosplayed) by (yourr) work.

CHART 2
ERROR-ANALYSIS CHART
(Top Half)

The Error-Analysis Chart on page 10 provides you with an analysis of your individual typing weaknesses and tells you what to do to correct them. If you carefully fill out this chart after taking a 5-minute timing, you will immediately know which error patterns are causing you difficulty.

Assume that the passage below was typed as part of Timed Writing 1. Refer to the passage below and Sample Chart 2 on page 5 as you study the steps in completing the top half of Chart 2. (The circled numbers on the sample chart correspond to the steps.) If a word has more than one error, only the first error is counted and recorded.

Steps in Completing Top Half of Chart 2

1. Record misstrokes by writing the letter that you struck in error in the box under the letter that you should have struck. (The letters are arranged according to which finger controls the letter.) You may have to write more than one letter in the same box.

Example: In line 1 of the passage, in the word *is*, the letter *l* was struck in error for the letter *s*. You would therefore write the letter *L* in the box under the letter *S*.

2. Record each punctuation, shifting, and spacing error by placing a dot in the appropriate box for each occurrence.

Example: In line 1 of the passage, the *t* in *Typing* was not capitalized and the words *ways of* were typed without a space separating them. In line 2, the word *you* was improperly capitalized and the *period* was struck in error for the comma. You would therefore place two dots in the shifting box, one in the spacing box, and one in the punctuation box.

3. Record each error caused by a lack of concentration by placing a dot in the box in the concentration column.

Concentration errors include adding a letter or word, omitting a letter or word, transposing letters or words, or doubling the wrong letter.

Example: In line 2 of the passage, the word *will* has the wrong letter doubled, the letters of the word *the* were transposed, and the letter *r* has been omitted in the word *produced.* In line 3, a letter has been added to the word *your.* You would therefore put four dots in the concentration column.

4. Count the number of errors made by each finger of the left hand, and write the number in the appropriate boxes in the columns labeled "Left-Hand Error Summary." Then write the total left-hand errors in the column labeled "Total Left."

Example 1: One error was made on a letter controlled by the third finger of the left hand—1 error on the letter *s.* You would write the digit *1* in the 3d Finger column.

Example 2: Four errors were made on letters controlled by the first finger of the left hand—1 error on the letter *g,* 1 error on the letter *r,* and 2 errors on the letter *t.* You would write *4* in the 1st Finger column.

Example 3: In all, 5 errors were made involving the left hand. You would write *5* in the column labeled "Total Left."

5. Using the same procedures as you did for the left-hand summary, complete the columns labeled "Right-Hand Error Summary."

6. Count the total number of errors made in the timed writing, and write the number in the box in the column labeled "Total Errors."

Example: In the passage below, 15 errors were made: 5 left-hand errors, 2 right-hand errors, 1 punctuation error, 2 shifting errors, 1 spacing error, and 4 concentration errors. You would therefore write the number *15* in the last column.

EXERCISE: Based on the errors circled on the Timed Writing 1 sample (page 3), complete the top half of the sample of Chart 2 on page 3. Check your work with the key on page 12.

TW NO.	L‑4th	L‑3d	L‑2d	L‑1st	Tot. Lt.	Q	A	Z	W	S	X	E	D	C	R	F	V	T	G	B	Y	H	N	U	J	M	I	K	O	L	P	R‑1st	R‑2d	R‑3d	R‑4th	Tot. Rt.	Punct. Errors	Shifting Errors	Spacing Errors	Concentration Errors	Total Errors
LEFT‑HAND ERROR SUMMARY / FINGER →						**LEFT‑HAND KEYS** →															**RIGHT‑HAND KEYS** →											**RIGHT‑HAND ERROR SUMMARY / FINGER** →									
1		1		4	5					L					Y/R	F		T						U					O					1	1	2	•	•••		••	15

Circled sequence guides printed between the halves: ④ (under Finger left summary), ① (under left keys), ⑤ (under right summary), ② ③ ⑥ (under punctuation / concentration / total).

	L‑4th	L‑3d	L‑2d	L‑1st	Tot. Lt.	Q	A	Z	W	S	X	E	D	C	R	F	V	T	G	B	Y	H	N	U	J	M	I	K	O	L	P	R‑1st	R‑2d	R‑3d	R‑4th	Tot. Rt.	Punct.	Shift.	Space	Concentr.	Total
Max. Errors Allowed	1	2	2	3	4	1	1	1	1	1	1	1	1	1	1	1	1	1	1	1	1	1	1	1	1	1	1	1	1	1	1	3	2	2	1	4	1	1	1	2	5
Accuracy Study	17	15	13	11	19	17	1	26	23	19	24	5	4	3	18	6	22	20	7	2	25	8	14	21	10	13	9	11	15	12	16	12	14	16	18	20	21	10	9		7
Pages	65‑66	64	62‑63	59‑60	67‑68	55	52	57	56	55	56	53	53	53	55	53	56	56	53	53	56	54	55	56	54	54	54	54	55	54	55	61‑62	63‑64	65	66	68	69‑70	58‑59	57‑58	*	51‑52
PL	3	3	3	3	5	5	5	5	5	5	5	5	5	5	5	5	5	5	5	5	5	5	5	5	5	5	5	5	5	5	5	3	3	3	3	5	3	3	10		3
Wk 1				4	5													2																			3		1	6
Wk 2																																								
Wk 3																																								
Wk 4																																								
Wk 5																																								

(The Accuracy Study line is labeled across the key columns: "ACCURACY STUDY 8/Drill No.")

CHART 2 ERROR-ANALYSIS CHART (Bottom Half)

The bottom half of the Error-Analysis Chart provides your prescriptive practice exercises and allows you to keep a record of all corrective practice that must be completed for the week. The first line of the bottom half of Chart 2 shows the maximum number of errors that can be made for any category (strokes, fingers, hands, and so on). The second line of the chart indicates what accuracy study to do. The third line of the chart gives the page number(s) of the study. The fourth line of the chart, labeled "PL" (perfect lines), indicates how many perfect lines of each drill you should type. The next five lines, labeled "Wk 1" to "Wk 5," are where you will keep a record of what drills you have to type each week.

Only errors made on 5-minute *Pretests* require corrective practice drills, so only those errors are recorded on the bottom half of Chart 2. However, you should fill out the top half of Chart 2 for all 5-minute timings in order to compare them with the most recent Pretest. The timed-writing numbers that are shaded in Chart 2 are the Pretests. Corrective practice is necessary following the Pretest timings. Therefore, completing the bottom half of Chart 2 is *essential*.

Steps in Completing Bottom Half of Chart 2

1. For each column of Chart 2, compare the number of errors you made with the maximum number of errors allowed (first line of bottom half of Chart 2). Since you exceeded the maximum number of errors allowed for the first finger of the left hand, total left, as well as for the T key, shifting errors, concentration errors, and total errors, you automatically know that corrective practice is necessary.

2. Assume that the sample passage is from the Pretest for the first week. Therefore, all drill work to be done would be recorded on the Wk 1 line. Place a dot in each column where you exceeded the maximum errors allowed.

Example: The first finger of the left hand requires a dot in the 1st Finger column of the Left-Hand Error Summary on the Wk 1 line. Continue in the same manner for all the other errors in which you exceeded the maximum amount.

3. Corrective practice drills are to be typed in the following sequence: (1) concentration drills; (2) letters of the alphabet; (3) punctuation, shifting, and spacing; (4) fingers; (5) hands; (6) total errors. This sequence appears on the actual chart as a visual reminder.

Example: The corrective practice for the sample passage would be typed in the following sequence: (1) concentration; (2) T key; (3) shifting errors; (4) first finger of the left hand; (5) total left hand; (6) total errors.

4. On the first line below the PL line, the Wk 1 line, you will record the sequencing of the corrective practice drills over the dots you previously made.

Example: You will place a *1* in the concentration box, a *2* in the letter T box, a *3* in the shifting box, and so on.

Note: Because the concentration drills vary from week to week and space is limited in Chart 2, an asterisk is shown in the concentration column which refers to the scale to the right of Chart 2. Be sure to follow those assignments if you make three or more concentration errors.

Steps in Completing the Drills

As discussed earlier, corrective practice drills are to be done in a specific sequence. Since you already did your prioritizing on Chart 2, it will be easy for you to begin.

1. Within each drill type, the sequence should be in accordance with the number of errors made.

Example: If you made 3 errors on the T key and 2 errors on the S key, you would type the T drills before the S drills.

2. Once a drill has been satisfactorily completed, draw an "X" through the box, so you know which drills you have done as well as which ones remain to be done.

3. At the end of the week you will take a Posttest. This portion of the Posttest (the 5-minute timing) is similar to the Pretest.

Note: Do not begin the corrective practice based on Chart 2 until you have filled out Chart 3, unless the teacher has advised you otherwise.

EXERCISE: Based on the top half of Chart 2, complete the bottom half of the sample of Chart 2 on page 3. Check your work with the key on page 12.

CHART 3
SPEED AND ACCURACY ANALYSIS

The Speed and Accuracy Analysis on page 11 will enable you to determine your strengths and weaknesses in making various stroke combinations with regard to both speed and accuracy. You accomplish this by taking ten 1-minute timings on individual sentences—every ten sentences is one diagnostic test. Each sentence is specially constructed to emphasize a certain stroke combination (for example, vertical strokes or one-hand words). Since the page numbers and number of perfect lines are given at the bottom of Chart 3 for each sentence of the speed and accuracy studies, you can easily locate the drills you should practice to correct any weaknesses uncovered. Follow Sample Chart 3 on page 7 in filling out Chart 3.

Steps in Completing Chart 3

1. As part 2 of the Pretest, take a 1-minute timing on each of the ten sentences from one of the sets of diagnostic tests in Section 4. On diagnostic tests, push for speed with accuracy. Figure your correct words a minute (CWAM) and error scores on each sentence and enter the scores in the appropriate boxes of the Pretest columns.

Note: To compute your CWAM, subtract one word from your gross speed for each error made.

Example: Assume that you typed 47 words a minute on Sentence 1 and made 4 errors. Your CWAM would be 43 $(47 - 4 = 43)$. You would therefore write the number 43 in the CWAM box and the number 4 in the upper half of the Errors box for Sentence 1.

2. Refer to the sample table on page 7. This table shows the minimum CWAM speeds you should be achieving on each of the 1-minute timings. The speeds vary for each of the sentences based on the degrees of difficulty of the various stroke combinations. To know which column of this table to use, turn back to Chart 1 and determine your GWAM speed on the first 5-minute Pretest you took. Round this number off to the nearest 5. The resulting number will tell you which column of the table to use to see how fast you should be typing for each 1-minute timing. Write the minimum speeds from the column in the boxes labeled "Minimum" in the Pretest columns of Chart 3.

Example: Assume that your first GWAM score on your 5-minute Pretest was 38. Rounding this number off to the nearest 5 would give you 40. You would therefore write the numbers from the 40 column (46, 41, 46, and so on) in the appropriate Minimum boxes of the Pretest columns.

3. For each timed writing, compare the CWAM speed you actually made with the minimum speed you should have made. If your speed was less than the minimum, write the difference between the scores in the upper half of the box labeled "Deficiency." If your speed was higher than the minimum, leave this box blank.

Example: On Sentence 1 your actual speed was 43 but the minimum speed was 46. Since your actual speed was 3 words less than the minimum speed required, you would write the number 3 in the upper half of the Deficiency box. On Sentence 2 your actual speed was 45 but the minimum speed was 41. Since your speed was higher than the required minimum speed, you would leave this box blank.

ITEM		Sentence 1		Sentence 2		Sentence 3	
		PRE	POST	PRE	POST	PRE	POST
Diagnostic Test 1	Errors	④/2		⑤/1		3/	
	Minimum	46		41		46	
	CWAM	43		45		42	
	Deficiency	3/2		—		4/1	
Diagnostic Test 2	Errors						
	Minimum						
	CWAM						

Sentence No.	Feature	20	25	30	35	40	5-M 45
1	Simple vocabulary	26	31	36	41	46	52
2	High-stroke intensity	22	27	32	36	41	46
3	Alternate hand	26	31	36	41	46	51
4	Compound strokes	24	29	35	40	46	52
5	Vertical strokes	18	23	28	33	38	43
6	Double letters	20	25	30	35	40	47
7	One-hand words	18	23	28	33	38	44
8	Alphabetic	20	25	30	35	40	47
9	Frequent spacing	28	33	38	43	48	54
10	Frequent shifting	10	14	18	22	28	34

4. Every timed writing for which you have a number written in the upper half of the Deficiency box indicates that you need extra *speed* practice on that particular stroke combination.

5. Every sentence in which you made more than 3 errors indicates that you need extra *accuracy* practice on that particular stroke combination. Draw a circle around any numbers above 3.

Example: Since you made 4 errors in Sentence 1, circle the number in that box.

6. Once you have eliminated all speed deficiencies or have no more than one speed deficiency on the Pretest, you are automatically promoted to the next higher speed column.

7. At the end of the week you will take a Posttest. This portion of the Posttest (the diagnostic test) is on the same material as the Pretest. Repeat Step 1 and record your scores in the Posttest column to rate your gains in speed and accuracy.

Completing the Corrective Practice

First do the corrective practice based on Chart 2. Then do the Chart 3 accuracy study drills before proceeding to the speed study drills. Always begin the corrective practice (for both the accuracy and speed studies) on the sentences that have the highest number of errors and then the highest speed deficiencies. Space is provided in the lower half of the Errors and Deficiency boxes to sequence your corrective practice.

1. As mentioned earlier, the number of each sentence is the same as the study number that emphasizes that particular stroke combination. Therefore, you will immediately know which accuracy and/or speed studies to go to.

Further instructions on completing these drills will be explained at the beginning of each study.

2. With each drill type, the sequence should be in accordance with the number of errors made.

Example 1: On Diagnostic Test 1, 4 errors were made on Sentence 1 and 5 errors were made on Sentence 2. Place a *1* in the lower half of the Errors box for Sentence 2 and a *2* in the lower half of the Errors box for Sentence 1, indicating that you would type the accuracy studies for Sentence 2 before doing the accuracy studies for Sentence 1.

Example 2: On Diagnostic Test 1, a speed deficiency of 3 was made on Sentence 1 and a speed deficiency of 4 was made on Sentence 3. Place a *1* in the lower half of the Deficiency box for Sentence 3 and a *2* in the lower half of the Deficiency box for Sentence 1, indicating that you would type the speed studies for Sentence 3 before doing the speed studies for Sentence 1.

3. To indicate that you have finished a study, draw an "X" through the numbers.

EXERCISE: Review the Diagnostic Test 1 sample on page 8. With the information given, complete the sample of Chart 3 on page 8. Use the GWAM on the sample timing in Chart 1 on page 3.

In summary, the cycle is as follows: (1) Take a Pretest, which consists of two 5-minute timings and one diagnostic test. (2) Complete Charts 1, 2, and 3. (3) Do the corrective practice according to the results of your Pretest. (You may also do the 1-minute timings on the skill-development paragraphs on the corrective practice days.) (4) At the end of the week take a Posttest. Compare the Pretest and Posttest results to note your gains in speed and accuracy.

SAMPLE EXERCISE 3

Diagnostic Test 1

See if we can go and (hlp) them to do a fine job for the men and women.
See if we can go and help them to (to) a fine job for the men and women.
See if we can go and help them to do a fine job for the men and women.

Hostile conditions on the peninsula dissuaded (thim) from the (adventere.)
(hostile) conditions on the peninsula (dissuadde) them from the adventure.
Hostile conditions on the peninsula dissuaded

Their neurotic visitor may burn down the five docks if he is not paid.
Their neurotic visitor may burn down the five docks if he is not paid.

The pure vein of our silver was more than we had anticipated at first.
The pure (veen) (ofour) silver was more than we had anticipated at first.
The pure vein of our silver was more than we had anticipated at first.

My annual bazaar grew swiftly and dazzled many overburdened lobbyists.
My annual (bazar) grew swiftly and dazzled many overburdened lobbyists.
My annual

The bookkeeping committee (frim) Tennessee embarrassed a (fottball) coach.
The bookkeeping committee from Tennessee (embarassed) a football coach.
The (bookkepping) committee from Tennessee embarrassed a football coach.

My nylon dress was the best garb she could wear to the bazaar at noon.
My nylon dress was the best garb she could wear to the bazaar at noon.
My (nulon)

A quick movement of the bold enemy will jeopardize six good divisions.
A quick movement of the bold enemy will jeopardize six good divisions.
A quick movement of the

I am to see if (i) am to do it now or if he is to do it at a later time.
I am to see if I am to (to) it now or if he is to do it at a later time.
I am to see if I am (todo) it now or if he is to do it at a later time.
I am to see (ef) (i) am to do it now or if he

It Is The Duty Of A King To Do Me A Turn If He Can And He Is To Do So.
It Is The

| 1 | 2 | 3 | 4 | 5 | 6 | 7 | 8 | 9 | 10 | 11 | 12 | 13 | 14

Sentence No.	Feature	20	25	30	35	40
1	Simple vocabulary	26	31	36	41	46
2	High-stroke intensity	22	27	32	36	41
3	Alternate hand	26	31	36	41	46
4	Compound strokes	24	29	35	40	46
5	Vertical strokes	18	23	28	33	38
6	Double letters	20	25	30	35	40
7	One-hand words	18	23	28	33	38
8	Alphabetic	20	25	30	35	40
9	Frequent spacing	28	33	38	43	48
10	Frequent shifting	10	14	18	22	28

CHART 3   SPEED AND ACCURACY ANALYSIS

	ITEM	Sentence 1		Sentence 2		Sentence 3		Sentence 4		Sentence 5		Sentence 6		Sentence 7		Sentence 8		Sentence 9		Sentence 10	
		PRE	POST	PRE	POST	PRE	POST	PRE	POST	PRE	POST	PRE	POST	PRE	POST	PRE	POST	PRE	POST	PRE	POST
Diagnostic Test 1	Errors																				
	Minimum																				
	CWAM																				
	Deficiency																				

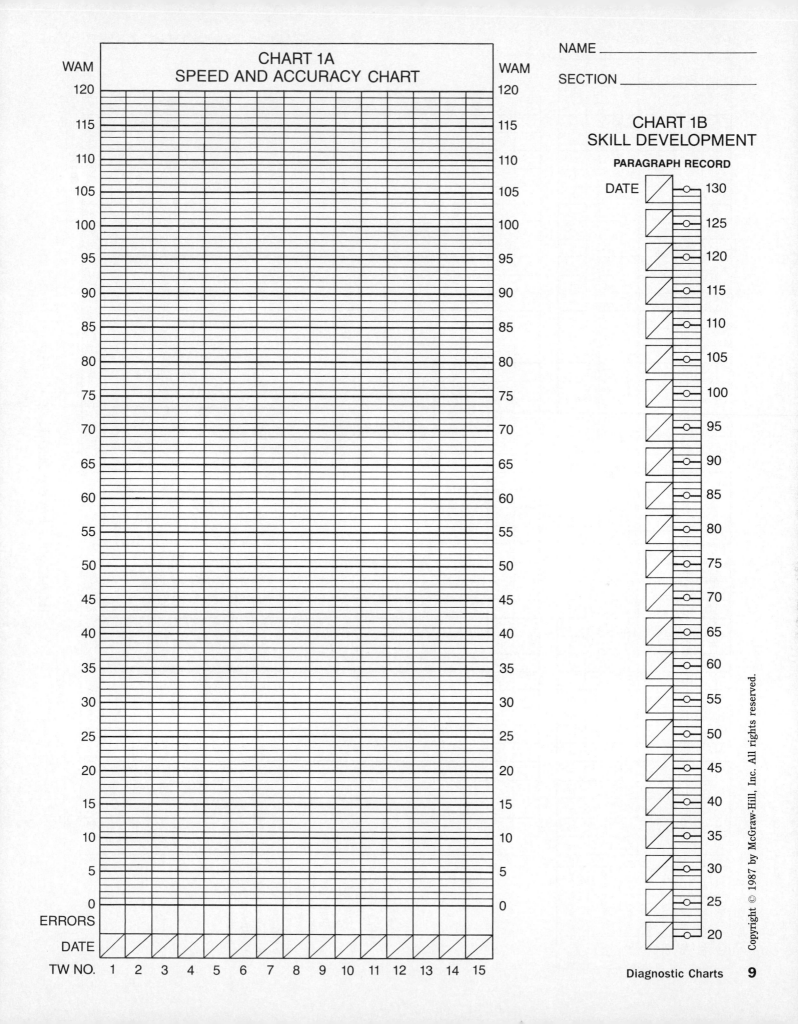

CHART 2   ERROR-ANALYSIS CHART

NAME _____   SECTION _____

The main grid records errors per **TW NO.** (rows 1–15) across the following column groups:

TW NO.	LEFT-HAND ERROR SUMMARY (FINGER)					LEFT-HAND KEYS															RIGHT-HAND KEYS											RIGHT-HAND ERROR SUMMARY (FINGER)					Punctuation Errors	Shifting Errors	Spacing Errors	Concentration Errors	Total Errors
	4th	3d	2d	1st	Tot. Lt.	4th Finger			3d Finger			2d Finger			1st Finger						1st Finger						2d Finger		3d Finger		4th Fin.	1st	2d	3d	4th	Tot. Rt.					
						Q	A	Z	W	S	X	E	D	C	R	F	V	T	G	B	Y	H	N	U	J	M	I	K	O	L	P										

(Shaded TW rows: 1, 3, 5, 8, 11. Data cells blank.)

Sequence of Corrective Practice Drills

1. Concentration
2. Letters of the Alphabet
3. Punctuation, Shifting, and Spacing
4. Fingers
5. Hands
6. Total Errors

ACCURACY STUDY 8 / Drill No. (cross-reference: Accuracy Study, Drill No., Pages, PL, Max. Errors Allowed)

Key / Category	Max. Errors Allowed	Accuracy Study 8	Drill No.	Pages	PL
Q	1	17	1	55	3
A	1	1	26	52	3
Z	1	23	19	57	3
W	1	24	5	56	5
S	1	18	6	55	5
X	1	22	20	56	5
E	1	7	2	53	5
D	1	25	8	53	5
C	1	14	21	53	5
R	1	10	13	55	5
F	1	9	11	53	5
V	1	15	12	56	5
T	1	16	—	56	5

Punctuation / Shifting / Spacing / Concentration / Total Errors

Category	Max. Errors Allowed	Pages	Drill No.	PL
Punctuation Errors	1	61–63, 62–64	12, 14	3, 3
Shifting Errors	1	65	16	3
Spacing Errors	1	66	18	3
Concentration Errors	2	68	20	5
Total Errors	1	69–70	21	3
	1	58–59	10	3
	1	57–58	9	10
	2	*		
	5	51–52	7	5

Accuracy Study (weekly)

	Max. Errors Allowed	Accuracy Study	Pages	PL	Wk 1	Wk 2	Wk 3	Wk 4	Wk 5
	17	1	65/66	3					
	15	2	62/64	3					
	13	2	62–63	3					
	11	3	59–67/60	3					
	19	4	68	5					

Diagnostic Charts 10

* Concentration Drills

Wk	Pages	PL
1	71–74	3
2	75–76	2
3	77–79	2B**
4	80–81	3B
5	82–83	2B

**B = Backwards

CHART 3 SPEED AND ACCURACY ANALYSIS

NAME _____   SECTION _____

	ITEM	Sentence 1 PRE	POST	Sentence 2 PRE	POST	Sentence 3 PRE	POST	Sentence 4 PRE	POST	Sentence 5 PRE	POST	Sentence 6 PRE	POST	Sentence 7 PRE	POST	Sentence 8 PRE	POST	Sentence 9 PRE	POST	Sentence 10 PRE	POST
Diagnostic Test 1	Errors																				
	Minimum																				
	CWAM																				
	Deficiency																				
Diagnostic Test 2	Errors																				
	Minimum																				
	CWAM																				
	Deficiency																				
Diagnostic Test 3	Errors																				
	Minimum																				
	CWAM																				
	Deficiency																				
Diagnostic Test 4	Errors																				
	Minimum																				
	CWAM																				
	Deficiency																				
Diagnostic Test 5	Errors																				
	Minimum																				
	CWAM																				
	Deficiency																				
Studies	Accuracy	P. 42/5 PL		P. 43/5 PL		P. 45/5 PL		P. 46/5 PL		P. 47/3 PL		P. 50/5 PL		P. 51/3 PL		P. 52/5 PL		P. 57/10 PL		P. 58/3 PL	
	Speed*	P. 90		P. 92		P. 94		P. 96		P. 97		P. 98		P. 100		P. 101		P. 103		P. 104	

*In doing these speed assignments, first-semester students will type 3 PL of each, second-semester students will type 5 PL of each, and third- and fourth-semester students will type the prescribed number of lines indicated in the directions.

MINIMUM 1-MINUTE SPEEDS FOR DIAGNOSTIC TESTS

Sentence No.	Feature	5-Minute Timed Writing Speed—GWAM*																
		20	25	30	35	40	45	50	55	60	65	70	75	80	85	90	95	100
1	Simple vocabulary	26	31	36	41	46	52	59	66	74	81	88	93	98	103	108	113	118
2	High-stroke intensity	22	27	32	36	41	46	52	60	67	73	78	83	88	93	98	103	108
3	Alternate hand	26	31	36	41	46	51	56	62	68	74	80	86	92	97	102	107	112
4	Compound strokes	24	29	35	40	46	52	58	64	70	76	82	88	94	99	104	109	114
5	Vertical strokes	18	23	28	33	38	43	48	53	58	62	66	70	74	78	82	86	90
6	Double letters	20	25	30	35	40	47	54	58	62	66	70	73	76	82	87	92	97
7	One-hand words	18	23	28	33	38	44	51	55	60	64	68	71	74	80	85	90	95
8	Alphabetic	20	25	30	35	40	47	54	59	64	69	74	77	80	84	89	94	99
9	Frequent spacing	28	33	38	43	48	54	60	67	74	79	84	90	96	101	106	111	116
10	Frequent shifting	10	14	18	22	28	34	40	45	50	55	59	63	67	71	76	80	84

*Refer to Chart 1 for your GWAM speed on your first 5-minute timed writing and round off your speed to the nearest 5.

ANSWER KEY

CHART 1A

GWAM: 29 (144 ÷ 5 = 29)
ERRORS: 9
NWAM: 11 [29 − 18 (9 × 2) = 11]

ERRORS: 9

DATE

TW NO. 1 2 3 4 5 6

CHART 2

TW NO.	LEFT-HAND ERROR SUMMARY					LEFT-HAND KEYS																RIGHT-HAND KEYS											RIGHT-HAND ERROR SUMMARY					Punctuation Errors	Shifting Errors	Spacing Errors	Concentration Errors	Total Errors
	FINGER					4th Finger		3d Finger		2d Finger		1st Finger						1st Finger					2d Finger	3d Finger	4th Fin.	FINGER									
	4th	3d	2d	1st	Tot. Lt.	Q	A	Z	W	S	X	E	D	C	R	F	V	T	G	B	Y	H	N	U	J	M	I	K	O	L	P	1st	2d	3d	4th	Tot. Rt.					
1			2	2												J T											O						1			1	•	• •	•	• • •	9

Max. Errors Allowed	1	2	2	3	4	1	1	1	1	1	1	1	1	1	1	1	1	1	1	1	1	1	1	1	1	1	1	1	1	1	1	3	2	2	1	4	1	1	1	2	5
Accuracy Study	17	15	13	11	19	ACCURACY STUDY 8/Drill No.																										12	14	16	18	20	21	10	9		7
						17	1	26	23	19	24	5	4	23	18	6	22	20	7	2	25	8	14	21	10	13	9	11	15	12	16										
Pages	65-66	64	62-63	59-60	67-68	55	52	57	56	55	56	53	53	53	55	53	56	56	53	53	56	54	55	56	54	54	54	55	54	55	55	61-62	63-64	65	66	68	69-70	58-59	57-58	*	51-52
PL	3	3	3	5	5	5	5	5	5	5	5	5	5	5	5	5	5	5	5	5	5	5	5	5	5	5	5	5	5	5	5	3	3	3	3	5	3	3	10		3
Wk 1														2																										1	3

The 9 total errors include:

time.	punctuation
acheive	transposition/concentration
fijth	1st finger LH, F finger
NOrth	shifting
shealso	spacing
our at	transposition/concentration
ot	1st finger LH, F finger
forst	2d finger RH, I finger
corrdination	wrong letter doubled/concentration

DETERMINING CORRECTIVE PRACTICE

Box	Max. Errors Allowed	Errors Made	Drill Sequence
F key	1	2	2
Concentration	2	3	1
Total errors	5	9	3

CHART 3

	ITEM	Sentence 1		Sentence 2		Sentence 3		Sentence 4		Sentence 5		Sentence 6		Sentence 7		Sentence 8		Sentence 9		Sentence 10	
		PRE	POST	PRE	POST	PRE	POST	PRE	POST	PRE	POST	PRE	POST	PRE	POST	PRE	POST	PRE	POST	PRE	POST
Diagnostic Test 1	Errors	2		④	3	—		2		1		④	2	1		—		⑤	1	—	
	Minimum	36		32		36		35		28		30		28		30		38		18	
	CWAM	40		33		28		40		29		38		29		33		46		16	
	Deficiency	—		—		8	1	—		—		—		—		—		—		2	2

Sentence No.	Feature	20	25	30
1	Simple vocabulary	26	31	36
2	High-stroke intensity	22	27	32
3	Alternate hand	26	31	36
4	Compound strokes	24	29	35
5	Vertical strokes	18	23	28
6	Double letters	20	25	30
7	One-hand words	18	23	28
8	Alphabetic	20	25	30
9	Frequent spacing	28	33	38
10	Frequent shifting	10	14	18

1. The GWAM on the sample timing is 29; rounding off to nearest 5 is 30.
2. The numbers from the 30 column of the table are written in the appropriate Minimum boxes of the Pretest columns in Chart 3.
3. Any number above 3 in the Errors box is circled.

SECTION 2

CHAMPIONSHIP WARMUP DRILLS

Purpose: To develop fluency in making various stroke combinations.

Features: These drills contain a systematic arrangement of basic stroke combinations that are readily applicable to high-speed development in typing.

Line: 75 spaces

Directions: Type each drill ten times. Thereafter, type each line once daily as a warmup exercise. In typing these drills, try to curve your fingers and strike the keys with the fingertips without moving your arms or wrists. This is done by extending your fingers when reaching to the third row keys and by contracting your fingers when reaching to the first row. The proper stroking of the keys is essential to high-speed typing—*championship typing*—with excellent accuracy. These drills, many of which were used by the old typing masters, will reinforce proper stroking techniques.

Drill 1 (Each line contains 68 strokes.)

You Should Do Your Best Work At All Times To Make The Best Progress.
Typing Is Fun If You Type Well, And It Is Worth All Of Your Efforts.
Now And Then It Is True That We Can Do Well If We Want To Do So Now.
If We Enjoy Doing A Thing, We Do It As Well As It Is In Us To Do It.
It Is Up To You And Them To Find Out If He Is To Go To The Play Now.

Drill 2 (Each line contains 70 strokes.)

Put Your Best Effort Into Learning To Type And You Will Be Successful.
Do Your Best In Typing Each Day; You Will Be Pleased With The Results.
Now And Then It Is True That We Can Do More Than We Thought If We Try.
See If We Can Go With Them And Also Help To Do A Fine Job For The Man.
It Is The Duty Of An Aide To Do Me A Turn, And He Or She Should Do So.

Drill 3 (Each line contains 72 strokes.)

To Master The Drills Requires Excellent Timing With Marvelous Coordination.
Practice These Drills Faithfully, And You Will Be Pleased At Your Progress.
To Develop Fluency In Your Typing Is A Satisfying And Rewarding Experience.
It Is Very Encouraging To See Your Progress In Typing Continue Every Month.
This Is A Very Difficult Drill To Master, But You Are On The Way Right Now.

Drill 4 (Each line contains 75 strokes.)

You Should Be A Good Typist If You Follow The Paths Of Typing Champions.
Shifting Is Difficult, But You Will Succeed If You Will Continue To Try.
It Is We Who Will Have To Do Some Of The Things That We Will Not Do Now.
Now It Is Fine To Do Me A Turn And To Do It At A Time You Wish To Do So.
It Is Up To You And Me To See If It Is To Be As You And I Want It To Be.

DRILL 1

Second Row (Home Row) (66 strokes)

a;sldkfjghfjdksla;sldkfjghfjdksla;sldkfjghfjdksla;sldkfjghfjdksla;

DRILL 2

Second and Third Rows (68 strokes)

a;qpslwodkeifjrughtyfjrudkeislwoa;qpslwodkeifjrughtyfjrudkeislwoa;qp

DRILL 3

Second and First Rows (68 strokes)

a;z/slx.dkc,fjvmghbnfjvmdkc,slx.a;z/slx.dkc,fjvmghbnfjvmdkc,slx.a;z/

DRILL 4

Second, Third, and First Rows (72 strokes)

a;qpa;z/slwoslx.dkeidkc,fjrufjvmghtyghbnfjrufjvmdkeidkc,slwoslx.a;qpa;z/

DRILL 5

Second and Third Rows (68 strokes)

aq;pswlodekifrjugthyfrjudekiswloaq;pswlodekifrjugthyfrjudekiswloaq;p

DRILL 6

Second and First Rows (68 strokes)

az;/sxl.dck,fvjmgbhnfvjmdck,sxl.az;/sxl.dck,fvjmgbhnfvjmdck,sxl.az;/

DRILL 7

Third and Second Rows (68 strokes)

qap;wsoledikrfujtgyhrfujedikwsolqap;wsoledikrfujtgyhrfujedikwsolqap;

Drill 2 (Each line contains 73 strokes.)

It is up to you and him to see if it is to be as you and I want it to be.
I will do it if I have to do so but I am not in it for the fun of it now.
It is the big duty of a man to do me a turn if he can and he is to do so.
Now it is fine to do her a turn and to do it at a time you wish to do so.
It is she who will have to do some of the things that we will not do now.

Drill 3 (Each line contains 73 strokes.)

It is up to you and me to find out if I am to go to the city for it soon.
The man is to do as he is told if he is to make a fine job with the firm.
It is the duty of a scout to do a good deed each and every day if he can.
I am to go to the store to buy some pans for a fine time we plan to have.
If you wish to type well, you will type as well as it is in you to do it.

Drill 4 (Each line contains 75 strokes.)

See if it is to be as I say it is to be or if he is to do it as we like it.
If we like to do a task, we do it as well as it is in us to do it for them.
It is he who likes to run fast and he will run as fast as he can do so now.
You are to go to the zoo and play with the large boy if you can do so well.
It is fine to see our speed in typing grow and it is well worth the effort.

SPEED STUDY 10
FREQUENT-SHIFTING SENTENCES

Purpose: To develop fluency in using the shift key.

Features: These drill sentences contain a concentration of capital letters to compel frequent shifting. The sentences are arranged so that those requiring the most shifting are at the bottom of each drill and those requiring the least are at the top.

Drill Assignment: For Diagnostic Tests 1 to 4, use the drill that corresponds to the diagnostic test number. For Diagnostic Test 5, use Drills 1 and 4.

Line: 75 spaces

Directions: Type each line perfectly five times—not necessarily in succession, but in total—and double-space between groups of five perfect lines. Begin typing each sentence slowly, and gradually increase your typing rate as you become accustomed to the frequent shifting. Try to maintain an even typing tempo, while typing accurately. This is an exceedingly difficult and strenuous drill to type. Therefore, be prepared for some problems, which you will eventually overcome if you do not get too discouraged.

SECTION 3

5-MINUTE TIMINGS

Purpose: To develop speed and accuracy in typing ordinary straight copy for a period of 5 minutes.

Features: The subject matter will be of interest to you, and the copy contains an appropriate mixture of stroke patterns.

Line: 76 spaces

Note: Some lines have exactly 75 strokes, so if you add a stroke, you will have to strike the margin release key. Therefore, use a 76-stroke line.

Directions: Try not to exceed 5 errors on any 5-minute timing and type line for line. Your lines should begin and end exactly as they do in the book.

Drill 7 (Each line contains 75 strokes.)

A typing wizard just quickly amazed people before having to extend himself.
Very soon the boy will help make a lazy fox and quick weasel jump the gate.
The quick movement of five young elephants will jeopardize sixteen beagles.
A young, zealous Afghanistan expert very quickly believed the woman jurist.
New zigzag steps of a very quick jumping kangaroo exacerbated the old lion.

Drill 8 (Each line contains 75 strokes.)

Our black rabbits jumped over six puzzled, very white male fighting quails.
The audacity of my buzzard was shown when he quickly vexed a jumping moose.
The old Aztec viewed our king quizzically before expertly managing to jest.
My audience was amazed by the quick, very complete, extra-revealing report.
The professor's bleak quizzes vexed many ill-prepared junior college women.

SPEED STUDY 9
FREQUENT-SPACING SENTENCES

Purpose: To develop fluency in using the space bar.

Features: These sentences contain a preponderance of short words to compel frequent spacing. The sentences are arranged so that those with the greatest number of words are at the top of each drill and those with the least number are at the bottom. Spacing between words is one of the slowest strokes in typing; therefore, if you are to become a rapid typist, you must master the art of rapid spacing.

Line: 75 spaces

Drill Assignment: For Diagnostic Tests 1 to 4, use the drill that corresponds to the diagnostic test number. For Diagnostic Test 5, use Drills 1 and 4.

Directions: Type each line perfectly ten times—not necessarily in succession, but in total—and double-space between groups of ten perfect lines. Start typing each sentence slowly, and gradually increase your typing rate until you are typing as fast as you can. Try to maintain an even typing tempo between striking the keys and the space bar. In striving for speed, maintain a high degree of accuracy.

Drill 1 (Each line contains 70 strokes.)

I am to see if I am to do it now or if he is to do it at a later time.
It is the job of the man to help her if he can and he is to do it now.
If it is up to me to do it, I am not for it at this or any other time.
See if it is to be done now or if we can do it all in the near future.
Now and then it is true that we can do more than we thought if we try.

TIMED WRITING 1

During more than a quarter of a century, about ten thousand people   13
have learned the art of typewriting under my direct instruction. During   28
this period of time, there has not been one person who did not achieve this   43
facility, and this includes people from practically every background.   57

However, during my fifth year as an instructor, a young woman from   71
North Carolina entered our college. Her name was Ruth. She had been the   86
valedictorian of her high school class, and she also maintained an excel-   100
lent academic average at our school, except in the subject of typewriting.   115
It was my unfortunate duty to have to deny her a place on the honor roll   130
during her first year. She had the worst finger coordination imaginable.   145
It appeared that she could not get her fingers to cooperate with her mind.   160
Her self-respect was being slowly ground into oblivion. Yet she was one of   175
the hardest working students we had. Despite all the extraordinary efforts   191
she put forth, it seemed that day by day she fell further and further be-   205
hind the class.   209

At the end of the school year, this overly anxious young woman asked   222
if she would ever learn to type well. For the first time in my life there   237
was an overwhelming impulse to tell someone that it was absolutely hopeless   253
and there was little chance that she would become a good typist. Her eyes,   268
large with apprehension, demanded the assurance that she could make it.   282
Although she would need a fighting spirit to conquer her obvious obstacles   297
and would have to exert extra effort, a special program was outlined for   312
her to follow during the summer. She was admonished to apply herself com-   327
pletely to the task at hand as this would enhance her chances of success.   342

Not a defeatist by nature, Ruth practiced many hours each day during   356
the summer. No one knows how many hours, but it must have been a tremen-   370
dous number all together. When Ruth returned to college in the fall, she   385
not only had acquired excellent finger coordination but had developed a   399
considerable amount of speed and had achieved remarkable accuracy. At the   415
end of her second year, she received a gold medallion for being the out-   429
standing typist in the graduating class.   437

Here you have a story of a young woman who was at the bottom of her   451
class in typing the first year. However, she had an overwhelming desire to   466
be a good typist, and although she lacked the natural attributes, she   480
became the best in her class. So can you.   489

| 1 | 2 | 3 | 4 | 5 | 6 | 7 | 8 | 9 | 10 | 11 | 12 | 13 | 14 | 15

Drill 2 (Each line contains 67 strokes.)

Just four dozen boxes were moved quietly by carefully packing them.
Our famous gray squirrels jeopardized their very next black walnut.
Two black jets zipped quietly before many very highly waxed planes.
Their zebras jumped over six black squirrels following your trails.
Five or six cartons were awarded as equal major prizes by a knight.

Drill 3 (Each line contains 67 strokes.)

Mr. Quicke extrapolated the many hazards involved by joining waifs.
Your waltz quickly amazed Jeff and Steve plus excited bright folks.
Vabor's jasmine fragrance very quickly excels prize-winning aromas.
The very quaint woman just amazed Captain Vexoray by killing gnats.
Their five boxes of prunes quickly disquieted Thomas Z. Wright, Jr.

Drill 4 (Each line contains 68 strokes.)

Our weak jazz boys quickly consumed extra portions of light venison.
Just six dozen black fighters very quickly won prizes automatically.
Before subjecting the class to a quiz, Marke reviewed the xylophone.
The growing lack of jobs constitutes Quazady's major vexing problem.
Major Quinkploy was penalized five or six times because of fighting.

Drill 5 (Each line contains 68 strokes.)

Our zeal in typing will quickly justify vexing hand mobility drills.
The fighting men very quickly zipped the black wood with jaded axes.
Mazel proudly enjoyed quiet living and existing without fried bacon.
A quick lizard vexed a jumping fox until he pawed the yellow bricks.
Queen Kalexdrica just awarded the big prize to my vanquished father.

Drill 6 (Each line contains 70 strokes.)

A quick movement of the bold enemy will jeopardize six good divisions.
Extra work on psychology enabled five juniors to pass your major quiz.
The quiet preacher's texts just amazed forty very willing backsliders.
Zinnias, meekly vying for a bright effect, juxtaposed yellow jonquils.
The queer enzymes puzzled several exceptional judges before weakening.

Words

Life is not always a bowl of cherries. Sometimes it is very cruel, 14
and only a very strong, determined person is mentally and emotionally 28
equipped to overcome the hard knocks one experiences. Suffering and adver- 43
sity often strike without warning. This was true in the case of William, a 58
steady, rather studious young man. 65

William became an excellent typist after only one year of training in 79
this skill. In fact, he had achieved his personal goal in one year and 93
obtained a position as a clerk-typist. As this was the extent of his ambi- 108
tion, he dropped out of college. 115

About a year later, William telephoned to say that he had lost the use 129
of his right hand as the result of an automobile accident. In fact, he 144
could not move his right arm at all. It merely hung down by his side in a 159
seemingly lifeless manner. William had suffered a devastating experience, 174
and some fundamental changes would have to be made in his life-style to 188
enable him to adjust to the grim realities that were facing him. 201

He wondered if it were possible for anyone to learn to type by using 215
only one hand. Other handicapped individuals have achieved success in art, 230
music, and other professions, so the answer had to be in the affirmative. 245

William's eagerness astounded everyone. He was one of the first stu- 259
dents to register for the fall semester. From a psychological, physical, 274
and financial point of view, success was imperative. Learning the key- 288
board, inserting the paper, and turning pages in a book were only a few of 303
the minor obstacles facing this young man. The major problem was to de- 318
velop speed and accuracy comparable to what others could do with two hands. 333

William requested approval to take a concentrated typing course, and 347
in addition, he requested permission to practice during a three-and-a-half 362
hour interval between day and evening classes. Permission was granted, and 377
William practiced diligently and faithfully every single day. His dili- 391
gence and determination paid off, and by the end of the school year, he 406
passed a typing examination and got an excellent position. 418

At graduation, William received a gold medallion in recognition of his 432
extraordinary courage and display of perseverance. This incident from real 447
life should point out that a shattering blow need not destroy one but can 462
be a stepping-stone to other goals. William proved the proverb that says, 477
"Where there is a will, there is a way." If William could learn to type 492
with the use of only one hand, you can certainly learn to type too if you 506
will exert sufficient effort. 512

| 1 | 2 | 3 | 4 | 5 | 6 | 7 | 8 | 9 | 10 | 11 | 12 | 13 | 14 | 15

Drill 4 (Each line contains 70 strokes.)

The organized mink monopoly is the greatest fear of the wealthy women.

June was in a vegetated state, only minimally alive due to technology.

Some oily barges looked to be deserted of even minimum human activity.

An ill pupil fell into the oily pool as she dared to walk on its edge.

My nylon dress was the best garb she could wear to the bazaar at noon.

Drill 5 (Each line contains 72 strokes.)

Our popular people always pull the greatest gates at their best affairs.

The decedent had deeded an oil well to you a few weeks before his death.

A quick look at our lions deterred the pupil with polio from joining us.

An Egyptian mummy started a craze in archaeology that exceeded my hopes.

Minimum wages grew and grew steadily over the last decade in my opinion.

SPEED STUDY 8
ALPHABETIC SENTENCES

Purpose: To develop fluency in typing the entire alphabet.

Features: These sentences, each of which contains the 26 letters of the alphabet, are arranged in order of difficulty, with the least difficult at the top of each drill and the most difficult at the bottom.

Line: 75 spaces

Drill Assignment: For Diagnostic Tests 1 and 2, use the drill that corresponds to the diagnostic test number. For Diagnostic Test 3, use Drills 3 and 6; for Diagnostic Test 4, use Drills 4 and 7; for Diagnostic Test 5, use Drills 5 and 8.

Directions: Type each line perfectly ten times—not necessarily in succession, but in total—and double-space between groups of ten perfect lines. Begin typing each sentence at a slow rate of speed, and gradually increase your typing rate as you become more familiar with the sentence until you are able to type it at your most rapid accurate rate.

Drill 1 (Each line contains 62 strokes.)

The very quick typing expert just amazed our willing buffoons.

Two quick brown foxes jumped over the youngest sleeping zebra.

Their jazz expert can quickly manage to weave fabulous sounds.

Our six jumping zebras very quickly forced Harvey to withdraw.

Our lynx and zebra very quickly jumped over the wheezing frog.

Words

One of life's greatest pleasures is helping someone in need, espe- | 13
cially when the recipient really appreciates it. You, too, will find that | 28
nothing will give you a greater sense of satisfaction and achievement than | 43
knowing that you have used your knowledge, skill, and ability to help | 57
others to achieve a more pleasant and rewarding way of life. | 70

The story of Mildred is not unique. It is only one success story | 83
among many others that could be written about ambitious young people who, | 98
after being reared on a farm and experiencing deprivation, went to the city | 113
to seek either fame or fortune, or, in some instances, both. However, this | 128
is a true story of a young woman named Mildred, and her problems seemed | 142
unique to her. She was one of a large family of children and had lived on | 157
a farm all her life. In fact, she had never ventured far from home. No | 172
one in her family had ever attended college, and she wanted to be the | 186
first. | 188

When Mildred arrived in the city, she had no money, had no close | 202
friends, had no place to live, and had no one to provide financial assis- | 216
tance. She was completely on her own. However, Mildred possessed attri- | 231
butes that money cannot buy. She was resourceful, ambitious, and deter- | 245
mined to achieve her goal on her own. | 253

A preliminary test at our college showed that she was qualified for a | 267
junior position in both typing and shorthand. Her typing speed and short- | 282
hand skill enabled her, a novice, to work part-time for a local newspaper | 297
as a stenographer. Mildred earned sufficient income with this part-time | 311
job to enable her to attend school and provide for other necessities. She | 326
had no luxuries, as she earned only about two thousand dollars a year. | 341
This amount was just enough to make ends meet and pay her tuition. | 354

After Mildred graduated from college, she immediately went to work for | 368
a government agency. After a period of time, she transferred to another | 383
agency, then transferred to a position in the White House. After working | 398
at the White House, she had the opportunity to work overseas. She finally | 413
returned to America and now has a well-paying government position. | 427

The story of Mildred is a fascinating true story of a young woman who | 441
started on the lowest rung of the economic ladder, but advanced until she | 455
had a prestigious position and earned an excellent salary. | 467

There is no easy road to success, but you, too, will succeed if you | 481
utilize your capabilities properly and manage your resources and time. | 495

| 1 | 2 | 3 | 4 | 5 | 6 | 7 | 8 | 9 | 10 | 11 | 12 | 13 | 14 | 15

SPEED STUDY 7
ONE-HAND-WORD SENTENCES

Purpose: To develop fluency in typing one-hand words.

Features: These sentences contain a concentration of one-hand words and are arranged so that the sentences containing the least number of one-hand words are at the top of each drill, while those with a greater number of them are at the bottom.

Line: 75 spaces

Drill Assignment: Use the drill that corresponds in number with the diagnostic test number.

Directions: Type each line perfectly ten times—not necessarily in succession, but in total—and double-space between groups of ten perfect lines. Start typing each sentence slowly, and gradually increase your typing rate until you are able to type at your fastest accurate speed.

Drill 1 (Each line contains 65 strokes.)

Your deer veered in the field and retreated into the rear garage.

The tax rebates started the economy on an upturn as was assessed.

The desert fox was steadfast in his rear-guard retreat in Africa.

Our fat cat scattered garbage upon my garage floor and retreated.

A puny puppy chased a crazed cat in the grass area of the crater.

Drill 2 (Each line contains 67 strokes.)

The pink pin was not union made and badly ripped the nylon garment.

Their red bear was eager to tear the beehive down from the treetop.

Our jolly, bearded redhead jumped over the bag and tested your car.

Only our pumpkin and onion were the best in the opinion of experts.

Your dazed bear raged in his cage as a lion slyly looked on nearby.

Drill 3 (Each line contains 70 strokes.)

Your monopoly started the hula-hoop craze that swept our great nation.

The Arab oil embargo started a great gas fear that upset many nations.

His steadfast refusal to accede exceeded the opinion of our jolly dad.

Their eager pupil dared to weave an inky pattern upon sassafras paper.

Our ill-fed polo pony only stared at a puny onion in his filthy stall.

Words

The proper mental attitude is essential if one wishes to learn to   13
type. In fact, without the proper attitude, learning this skill will be   28
virtually impossible and a very difficult and frustrating experience.   42

When observing a champion type rapidly and apparently effortlessly,   56
one might well conclude that typing is a comparatively easy skill to ac-   70
quire. Appearances are tremendously deceptive in this respect. Perhaps   85
you can remember quite vividly the difficulty you had initially in learning   100
the typewriter keyboard. One needs only to study the conditions under   114
which the old masters perfected typing techniques to realize that it is   128
impossible to achieve success in typing without using the proper techniques   144
and without dedicated hard work. Histories of successful people--typists   158
and others--illustrate all too clearly the lessons of patience and the   173
efforts of years of practice and discipline.   182

However, typing does not have to be too difficult if you will learn   195
the right way to practice. In fact, the championship way you are now   209
studying is indeed the best way and the simplest way to learn to type. You   225
must realize that typing is a skill with many facets, and in order to ac-   239
quire this skill, you must use various and sundry practice procedures. The   254
proper typing techniques were developed by the old masters of typing over a   270
period of many years. These old masters made a very comprehensive study of   285
the various typing motions and developed the most expeditious way of making   300
every stroke and motion in typing. You are learning their methods, and if   315
you will follow instructions precisely, do exactly what you are told, and   330
type these drills faithfully and conscientiously, your success as an expert   345
typist is assured.   349

Another ingredient that is essential is absolute self-confidence. You   363
must assume that you are going to succeed in order to learn to type. One   378
of the surest ways to success in typing lies in thoroughness. This means   393
that you must decide that you are going to master typing, that you will   407
practice exactly as you are instructed, and that you will practice dili-   422
gently no matter how difficult it seems or how much time is required. In   436
typing, a regard for the small things is necessary. If you can overcome   451
small worries, you will soon override the greater obstacles you encounter.   466

It is true that some people become successful typists in less time   480
than others, but in every instance, putting in much hard work and develop-   493
ing the correct typing techniques guarantee success.   503

| 1 | 2 | 3 | 4 | 5 | 6 | 7 | 8 | 9 | 10 | 11 | 12 | 13 | 14 | 15

Drill 1 (Each line contains 60 strokes.)

Your summaries took a week to account for the missing items.
The buzzard puzzled and dazzled the bobbing, hopping rabbit.
A robber assassinated our careless ambassador in the ghetto.
Our letter will make it less difficult to find a bookkeeper.
A good queen will add class in running her official affairs.

Drill 2 (Each line contains 66 strokes.)

Your engineers assume that a discussion of stress will be helpful.
It appears that our supply of wrapped puzzles exceeded the demand.
A good broom will sweep the floor very clean at every opportunity.
The football rally filled the hall and helped in winning the game.
Your jazz rally really affected the jamming, skinny fiddle player.

Drill 3 (Each line contains 70 strokes.)

The computer programmer really communicated better after the occasion.
Our dollar bill today looks less stable as the international currency.
I recommend summarizing the communication to attract better attention.
The class quiz succeeded in getting a little better attention from us.
Our smaller malls will meet community demands sooner than bigger ones.

Drill 4 (Each line contains 72 strokes.)

A baggage official alleges that the supply of lizard skins is worrisome.
It appears, to my horror, that a terrible error will add to our problem.
The aberration embarrassed and deterred the sweet, opportunistic fellow.
Our bookkeeper struggled all week, under pressure, to balance his books.
Anne took the book and looked for a different summary to tell the class.

Drill 5 (Each line contains 75 strokes.)

Our groggy, staggering bullfighter assailed the old bull with all his fury.
An odd rabbit hopped a lizard, attacked a cabbage, and bobbed up your hill.
It is difficult for your bookkeeper to meet all committee rules officially.
My coffee connoisseur succeeded in accounting for the low supply of coffee.
A helpless raccoon successfully embarrassed an angry, aggressive bullmoose.

TIMED WRITING 5

Perseverance--the ability to persist despite obstacles, discourage- | 13
ment, frustration, and opposition--is a quality everyone who has learned to | 29
type well possesses. Do not become discouraged when you face days when you | 44
cannot get your fingers to react as you want them to do. Typing is a skill | 59
that presents countless opportunities for errors. A word may be omitted, | 74
letters interchanged, spaces skipped, or capitals missed. Somehow, though, | 89
if you will remember to economize your arm and body motions, use the tip of | 104
each finger to strike the keys, and keep your hands relaxed and your wrists | 119
steady and low, you will soon be on your way up the ladder to high-speed | 134
typing. | 135

Words are used to portray ideas and provide the reader with mental | 149
pictures. You will certainly have a feeling of accomplishment when you | 163
achieve the ability to think of words and your fingers react automatically | 178
and precisely by typing them perfectly and quickly. Just imagine for a | 192
moment that you are thinking ideas, and these ideas and thoughts are being | 207
immediately transmitted onto your paper as your fingers fly through the | 222
air, landing squarely and quickly on the correct keys. This marvelous | 236
experience and exhilarating feeling are well worth the many hours spent in | 251
acquiring this magnificent skill. | 258

To become an accurate, speedy typist is not as difficult as you might | 272
imagine. Yet you must persist in applying the proper typing techniques if | 287
you do not want to be trapped by poor posture, improper hand position, and | 302
incorrect fingering. Much of the strain of typing comes from improper | 316
finger motion and hesitation in locating the proper keys. Of equal impor- | 331
tance is being able to identify the particular problem you have in speed or | 346
accuracy development. The best way to discover these typing areas of weak- | 361
ness is by using the sophisticated diagnostic charts that are a part of | 375
championship typing. If you practice the weaknesses revealed, you will | 390
make rapid progress because you are concentrating your efforts on only | 404
those areas in which you are experiencing difficulty. | 415

Another way to regain your typing composure on a topsy-turvy day is to | 429
turn to the one-minute paragraphs and practice the first paragraph until | 444
you can type it perfectly in one minute. Then type another paragraph until | 459
you have perfected it in one minute, then another and another, until | 474
you have acquired mastery of the typewriter keyboard again. You will be | 488
amazed at how this method will enhance your typing ability. | 500

| 1 | 2 | 3 | 4 | 5 | 6 | 7 | 8 | 9 | 10 | 11 | 12 | 13 | 14 | 15

Drill 2 (Each line contains 68 strokes.)

The red lobsters broiled in a light-gray pot to the delight of many.
My immunologists decided that an outbreak of influenza was imminent.
The state ceded huge grants of hilly land to grumpy local officials.
A gray kibitzer frustrated the jury mumbling about his many junkets.
Your annual bazaar has grown swiftly as it dazzled many kind people.

Drill 3 (Each line contains 73 strokes.)

The mysterious nuclear threat numbs the logic of our grave deliberations.
An unusual buzzard survived a hazardous injury by reducing some activity.
That jazz celebrity blows sweet, melodious sounds that serenade humanity.
A tumultuous reception greeted the cynical mortgagee at the school plaza.
Two lobbyists jumped on the locomotive as it left the frenzied multitude.

Drill 4 (Each line contains 74 strokes.)

A sweet fragrance drifted through the fresh air and brought gratification.
Your azalea and mum bazaars attracted numerous friends from various areas.
An eccentric recluse decided to dedicate an aquaplane for his jolly nurse.
Your crafty grocer deeded a swamp to a brave graduate and tax-deducted it.
Their nylon umbrella overburdened the hungry celebrity eating gingerbread.

Drill 5 (Each line contains 75 strokes.)

The old nylon kimono softened a friend's frame and enhanced her appearance.
Many unnumbered aluminum targets have now been accumulated at the aquarium.
An old, grumpy grizzly bear grazed on cool grass and viewed lizards nearby.
The lonely mystic hugged a gregarious old Aztec and pledged his friendship.
A soliloquy brought a swelter of unkind, derisive grimaces from the colony.

SPEED STUDY 6
DOUBLE-LETTER SENTENCES

Purpose: To develop fluency in making double-letter strokes.

Features: These sentences contain a preponderance of double-letter words and are arranged so that the sentences containing the fewest number of double-letter words are at the top of each drill, while those containing a greater concentration of them are at the bottom. Double-letter strokes are among the slowest and most difficult stroke combinations in typing, especially at the high-speed level.

Line: 75 spaces

Drill Assignment: Use the drill that corresponds in number with the diagnostic test number.

Directions: Type each line perfectly ten times—not necessarily in succession, but in total—and double-space between groups of ten perfect lines. Begin typing each sentence slowly, and gradually increase your typing speed until you reach your fastest accurate rate.

TIMED WRITING 6

Individualists, all, are the thinkers and planners, the pioneers and | 14
leaders, who have dared to branch out into new experiences or perform exper- | 29
iments that have reshaped and changed our lives. Included in this group | 44
are those who developed and expanded expertise in the field of office | 58
skills, as well as inventors, scientists, and those in other fields. | 72

My father was both a pioneer and a leader in every sense. In addition | 86
to his fame as a champion typist, he was well known for his ability to mo- | 101
tivate others. Wherever he went, people who observed his demonstrations | 115
became so enamored they followed him from one demonstration to another | 130
and sometimes even followed him to Washington, D.C. Consequently, he was | 144
similar to the pied piper, except his music was played on the typewriter. | 159

After watching a demonstration in Atlantic City, a young man named | 173
Frank came to Washington with the idea of becoming the next world champion | 188
typist. In fact, before seeing my father type, he thought he was already | 203
the fastest typist in the world. Like so many people, he had been living | 217
in a world of fantasy. Success looked as if it were around the corner, but | 233
the corner just hadn't been turned. For the first time he realized that he | 248
needed championship coaching to advance step by step from basic typing | 262
skills into an entirely new realm--championship typing. | 273

Frank was typing about eighty net words a minute on ten-minute timed | 287
writings at that time. However, he had two serious flaws in his typing | 302
technique that prevented him from realizing his goal. First, he held his | 315
right hand too high. To an unknowledgeable person, this would not make any | 331
difference, but to a typing expert it was a terrible mistake. Second, he | 345
could not keep his elbows down. After typing two or three minutes, his | 360
elbows would slowly rise until his forearms would parallel the floor. This | 375
caused him to make extra errors and lose speed. Although Frank was deter- | 390
mined to excel in typing, the fact that he failed to perfect his typing | 404
techniques kept him from becoming a champion typist. | 415

Undoubtedly, you have unused resources that have never been recognized | 429
and talents that have never been used. But if you wish to make the best | 444
possible progress in typing, you must strive to use the proper techniques-- | 459
often called championship techniques. What may appear to be an insignifi- | 474
cant flaw in your technique can make the difference in how fast and how | 488
accurately you type. The decision is yours, but you must eliminate or | 502
overcome all obstacles that keep you from achieving the results you desire. | 517
It will not be easy, but it will certainly be worth the effort. | 530

| 1 | 2 | 3 | 4 | 5 | 6 | 7 | 8 | 9 | 10 | 11 | 12 | 13 | 14 | 15

Drill 4 (Each line contains 70 strokes.)

Work on your typing with daily regularity in a well-developed program.

I can find out what happened if you fail to pick up the last ten boys.

The ship sailed out of the port into the open sea without the captain.

To ignore the methods of typing champions will lead you to mediocrity.

The good personality of the girl helped make her a very famous person.

Drill 5 (Each line contains 71 strokes.)

He might take the option on the house if proper financing can be found.

One can endure rain quite well if one has the means to find a dry spot.

There might be more jobs for everyone in the country if we plan for it.

She may fail to cure a cold but a female may get well if she gets rest.

More and more boys and girls find that proficiency comes with practice.

SPEED STUDY 5
VERTICAL-STROKE SENTENCES

Purpose: To develop fluency in making vertical strokes. A vertical stroke is involved when two or more consecutive strokes are made by the same finger on different rows of the keyboard; for example, *my*, in which the *j* finger has to strike two keys consecutively on different rows of the keyboard.

Features: These sentences contain a concentration of vertical-stroke words and are arranged so that those sentences with the fewest number of vertical strokes are at the top of each drill, while those with the greatest number are at the bottom.

Line: 75 spaces

Drill Assignment: Use the drill that corresponds in number with the diagnostic test number.

Directions: Type each line perfectly ten times—not necessarily in succession, but in total—and double-space between groups of ten perfect lines. Begin typing each sentence slowly, and gradually increase your typing rate until you reach your maximum accurate typing speed.

Drill 1 (Each line contains 66 strokes.)

Our kickers injured and bruised their fragile frames in blizzards.

Any inhumane pledges decidedly portray some barbarism in humanity.

That braggart chews his fresh, sweet fruit and bows to his granny.

The craft drifted swiftly with the smooth flow of the muddy brook.

A very cold swan swiftly swam the brook to celebrate its birthday.

Words

Typing training is a great developer of character. It requires a mix-   14
ture of pliability, perseverance, discipline, and honesty to achieve this   29
important motor skill. You must develop all these characteristics if you   44
wish to master and excel in typing. It also takes a great deal of human   58
intelligence and human will to apply the basic mechanics. Typing is not an   73
easy skill, and to achieve success, you must set realistic goals. You may,   89
after an honest self-analysis, be compelled to admit that your goals need   103
to be redefined.   107

You must educate yourself both in class and out of class. Typing   120
skill is not free. It is not something you receive or have presented to   134
you as a gift. The only way in which you can obtain it is to want it   148
enough to pay for it with your own efforts. You must earn this skill, just   164
as you must earn everything else that is really valuable to you.   176

You, more than anyone else, determine how fast you will acquire typing   191
proficiency. No matter how much and how well you are taught, no matter   205
what opportunities you have for learning, you will gain almost nothing   219
unless you take an active interest in remedying your deficiencies. These   234
timed writings will reveal your strong points and your weak points and will   249
emphasize what you need to practice to gain proficiency.   261

A real desire to learn serves as a "self-starter." It will give you a   275
driving purpose toward a definite goal. It will keep your mind wide awake   290
and make practice interesting, and even exciting. Without waiting to be   305
taught, you should make every effort to attain mastery of this important   320
skill. If, in addition to wanting to learn, you have gained skill in man-   335
aging yourself and your time and in disciplining your mind, you will make   349
very rapid progress.   354

Unfortunately, some students lack skill in typing because they have   367
not trained themselves to study efficiently. You cannot plod rather   381
blindly through crucial typing assignments day after day and hope to make   396
spectacular progress. If you muddle along--wasting your time and energy--   410
you will become discouraged. It is imperative that you study proper skill-   425
development strategies.   430

Frustrations are a part of becoming an expert typist. To attain typ-   444
ing proficiency, your fingers must respond automatically to the impulse of   459
your brain. If you will dedicate yourself to a high standard of perfection   474
in your practicing, you will soon be transformed into a superior typist.   489

| 1 | 2 | 3 | 4 | 5 | 6 | 7 | 8 | 9 | 10 | 11 | 12 | 13 | 14 | 15

SPEED STUDY 4
COMPOUND- AND MULTIPLE-STROKE SENTENCES

Purpose: To develop fluency in making compound- and multiple-stroke combinations. A compound stroke is one in which two or more consecutive strokes are made by two or more different fingers of the same hand; for example, the word *not*, in which the letters *no* are struck by two different fingers of the right hand. A multiple stroke takes place when two compound strokes in one word involve two or more fingers of one hand and, then, two or more fingers of the other hand. Example: *more*, which involves two fingers of the right hand, followed by two fingers of the left hand. You can develop tremendous typing speed by mastering compound and multiple strokes.

Features: These sentences contain a preponderance of compound- and multiple-stroke words. The sentences are arranged so that those with the greatest number of compound strokes are at the top of each drill and those with the least number are at the bottom.

Line: 75 spaces

Drill Assignment: Use the drill that corresponds in number with the diagnostic test number.

Directions: Type each line perfectly ten times—not necessarily in succession, but in total—and double-space between groups of ten perfect lines. Start typing each line slowly, gradually increasing your typing rate on each line until you are able to type at your maximum accurate speed.

Drill 1   (Each line contains 66 strokes.)

The pure vein of silver was more than we had anticipated at first.

We find that our view is not in harmony with that of some friends.

Now and then he could pick out a fine tune on his brand new piano.

Josie can hit the ball hard if it is pitched to her favorite spot.

The lure of the lost wilds called many boys and men to a new life.

Drill 2   (Each line contains 67 strokes.)

Whether we find more shops can make a big change in our selections.

He failed to find news about the job situation in his own hometown.

The paint can be picked off the post daily and thrown into the pit.

He might view the situation with some concern, but for his options.

One must try to do the best work every day to win fame and fortune.

Drill 3   (Each line contains 68 strokes.)

The piano will last as long as the quiet boy plays it in a fine way.

No one can find out more about the future than by studying the past.

Diagnostic typing can enable you to improve your speed and accuracy.

The girl displayed poise as she went on her way home that sunny day.

Be sure that when you practice typing, you do it with a lot of zest.

TIMED WRITING 8

Despite opinions to the contrary, American Indians, of necessity,   13
lived very systematic lives. The men had certain functions and duties to   28
perform just as the women had their places of responsibility. The fall and   43
winter months were the busiest times of the year. During the fall the In-   58
dians were busy gathering wild vegetables to be used during the cold winter   73
months. In addition, they were occupied with restoring garments or making   88
new clothing and with handcrafting weapons for use in the winter hunting.   103

The Plains Indians depended chiefly on hunting for their food supply.   117
The regions teemed with wildlife--wild geese and ducks, prairie chickens,   132
turkeys, deer, and many other kinds of game. But by far the most important   147
game was buffalo. Each year the Indians killed thousands of buffaloes for   162
meat, clothing, bowstrings, harnesses, and tents. However, they killed   177
only what was needed. There was no indiscriminate slaughter.   189

Before starting on the winter hunt, the Indian chiefs and their braves   204
had to be in top physical condition. They needed tremendous stamina and   218
endurance to face the blizzards they were sure to encounter. With infinite   233
patience, these men, wearing snowshoes to aid their mobility, followed   248
footprints the animals made in the snow, until they overtook their prey.   262

Their picturesque homes, called tepees, were made of skins that were   276
placed on poles and had the appearance of giant inverted cones. The   290
women did most of the work in the camp. They prepared the meals, kept the   305
tepee clean, skinned and cleaned the animals that had been brought in by   320
the hunters, and made clothes from the tanned skins of the animals.   334

Summer was considered the best time of the year. It was a time of   347
festivities and celebrations. During this relaxed time, everyone forgot   362
the hardships and miseries faced during the previous winter.   374

This was the time when a brave entered into courtship. In some Indian   388
tribes, the courtship ritual was a fascinating experience for all involved.   404
At midnight, a brave courting a maiden would go to the tepee where she   418
lived with her parents. He would light a splinter of wood and hold it in   433
front of her face as he awakened her. If the girl did not find him a   447
pleasing suitor, she would ignore the flame and let it burn. This was her   462
way of rejecting his proposal. If she liked him, she would blow out the   476
flame and he would ask her to become his wife. In an effort to gain the   491
acceptance of her parents, he would shower presents of blankets, ponies,   505
and other valuables upon them. Usually the parents consented if their   520
daughter wished to marry the brave.   525

| 1 | 2 | 3 | 4 | 5 | 6 | 7 | 8 | 9 | 10 | 11 | 12 | 13 | 14 | 15

Drill 1 (Each line contains 62 strokes.)

A giant whale is a sight to enchant the visitor and neighbors.
Henry cut the handle of the memento with an antique ivory pen.
The gowns of the girls dismayed the social clan of rich girls.
A busy, rich man got a big turkey and threw it some pale corn.
Bob wishes to augment their handiwork by the aid of ornaments.

Drill 2 (Each line contains 67 strokes.)

The boy wishes to fish with a rod in a dismal lake with a neighbor.
The prodigy is an authentic giant in the field of ancient toxicity.
Clemency may be a civic problem if it is not handled the right way.
Their auto burial firm pays fair prices for the worn autos it buys.
Eighty turkeys may make a big profit for busy Alan and his friends.

Drill 3 (Each line contains 69 strokes.)

He is to fix the auto panels and mend the hoses if he is to get paid.
Your neighbor is a bigot with a rigid view of what is right or wrong.
An unusual blend of fish and clams may fix a fair price for the meal.
The neurotic visitor may burn down the eight docks if he is not paid.
The lament of the pilots was a visible sight that saddened the world.

Drill 4 (Each line contains 71 strokes.)

Their ancient ivory emblem is an ornament to enrich and endow the city.
The height of the chapel may profit the land value of the neighborhood.
The big wolf makes a run for her lair and lays down with her pale cubs.
The authenticity of the proxy votes did torment the lame duck official.
If I focus on the dormant social problems, I will dismay our neighbors.

Drill 5 (Each line contains 73 strokes.)

The girl on a bicycle made a right angle turn on a busy lane in the city.
It is right to go to socials if they wish to mingle with their neighbors.
An ambush on the right flank of the corps may dismay their ill commander.
Did our neurotic neighbor enliven the sorority with her trivial problems?
Your auditor lays the blame for the penalties on a fiendish, bogus audit.

	Words

Time and again people came to our school for help after they had tried / 14
to gain expertise in typing and failed. This was true of Helen. For ten / 29
years after she graduated from high school, she went from school to school / 44
trying to learn to type well enough to get a position as a typist. Each / 59
time she was assured she would be successful and that it would be just a / 73
matter of time before she could type fast and accurately enough to qualify / 88
for a job. These promises all proved false, and in desperation she came to / 103
our school and asked if she were hopeless. / 112

This is not an unusual question after a history of ten years of trying / 126
and failing. However, before making any final judgment or drawing conclu- / 141
sions, we asked Helen to type for one minute in order that an analysis of / 156
her typing could be made. This was the real issue. / 167

After she had typed only two lines, her problems were obvious. Actu- / 180
ally, it was comparatively easy to analyze Helen's problems and prescribe / 195
the exact course that transformed her from a frustrated failure into a / 209
contented, hard-working student. She was given certain prescribed assign- / 224
ments that required diligent practice. Helen far exceeded the required / 239
practicing and willingly spent at least two to three hours each day prac- / 253
ticing at home in addition to the time spent in her class. There was a / 268
steady improvement, day by day, as she typed in class. Her whole attitude / 283
had changed from one of a defeatist to one of an optimist. Although there / 298
was an obvious struggle, she was on her way to becoming the successful / 312
typist of whom she had dreamed. / 318

About six weeks after she started, Helen was ready. She had mastered / 332
the assignments and had acquired the dexterity needed to pass the exami- / 347
nation. She arranged to take the test immediately, and the next day her / 361
smiling face verified that she had passed. No day in her life will be more / 377
momentous and seem of greater importance. Her persistence had paid off, / 391
and she had achieved the success she had sought for so many years. / 405

Helen's success, as yours, depended upon practicing in a certain pre- / 419
scribed manner. There just isn't any substitute for continual practicing / 433
in the correct manner. Practicing incorrectly only compounds your pro- / 448
blems. So attack each problem separately and repeat each problem area / 462
repeatedly until you eliminate the source of your difficulty. By consis- / 477
tently practicing in this manner you will soon find your fingers flying / 491
over the keyboard quickly and accurately. / 499

| 1 | 2 | 3 | 4 | 5 | 6 | 7 | 8 | 9 | 10 | 11 | 12 | 13 | 14 | 15

Drill 7 (Each line contains 73 strokes.)

Mastering the "art" of typing requires the application of motion studies.
Satisfaction is a pleasant personal experience derived from achievements.
Maintaining the character of a restaurant augments the proper atmosphere.
Your author's judgment in handling the disciplinary problem is erroneous.
Our traditional caloric indulgence at holiday time is a national problem.

Drill 8 (Each line contains 73 strokes.)

You can make outstanding progress by watching and listening to champions.
The gracious hospitality of the inhabitants enhanced the marvelous party.
A generation of companionship provided us insight into amiable relations.
Further significant information may conflict with our fundamental belief.
Specialized courtesy programs will enable our country to undergo changes.

Drill 9 (Each line contains 75 strokes.)

Listening to interesting neighbors is a wonderful way to enlarge your mind.
Ancient mariners would heed the guiding lighthouses on their homeward trek.
Everything important relating to your theory is awaiting our corroboration.
Their beautiful forefathers worshiped faithfully despite their adversities.
A knowledge of credit is desirable to alleviate serious financial problems.

Drill 10 (Each line contains 75 strokes.)

My country is in a precarious financial condition that necessitates action.
Their authority is concerned about maintaining excellent quality standards.
Everyone concluded that removing the chastised neighbor would be temporary.
Excellent progress in typing depends on quality skill-development programs.
Sundry individuals readily relate to others in similar positions of wealth.

SPEED STUDY 3
ALTERNATE-HAND SENTENCES

Purpose: To develop fluency in alternating hands while typing.

Features: These sentences contain a preponderance of alternate-hand words and are so arranged that those with the greatest number of alternate-hand words are at the top of each drill, while those with the least number are at the bottom.

Line: 75 spaces

Drill Assignment: Use the drill that corresponds in number with the diagnostic test number.

Directions: Type each line perfectly ten times—not necessarily in succession, but in total—and double-space between groups of ten perfect lines. Begin typing each line slowly; gradually increase your typing rate on each line until you are able to type as fast as you can with accuracy.

Words

A city is a study in contrasts. The rich, the poor, and the middle | 14
class dwell within its confines. Its varied architecture wears an air of | 29
confusion as an ultra-modern skyscraper rubs elbows with a Gothic cathe- | 43
dral, while across the street there is a parking lot with a wooden shed for | 58
the guard. And wide and splendid avenues cross undistinguished streets | 73
that dwindle off into back alleys. The city may seem cold and unfriendly, | 88
warm and enjoyable, an art center, a center of learning--it is all in the | 102
eye of the viewer. | 106

Actually it is all of these things and much more. A half hour's ride | 120
will transport one from the skyscrapers and crowds of the downtown area out | 136
to the farther reaches where small homes and lawns and vegetable gardens | 150
are just as much a part of the metropolis as downtown is. Elsewhere, the | 165
city may have a shoreline, with beaches and fishing and all the amenities | 180
of a fine summer resort. One has only to choose. | 190

And always and everywhere there's the traffic. The first-time visitor | 204
gazes incredulously at the cars, the buses, and the trucks moving bumper to | 219
bumper through the city. Even the sophisticated city dweller perks an ear | 234
in the direction of a siren on a fire truck or ambulance pursuing its | 248
intrepid way through snarls of traffic. | 256

During the day, the city is the shopper's paradise, the worker's bee- | 270
hive, the banker's countinghouse. Twilight turns the sidewalks and streets | 285
into a shadowy prairie stretching to the clifflike skyscrapers, and then | 300
the lights come on. Countless headlights and taillights in the roads | 314
shift and dart, the golden lights approaching, the red receding. | 327

Suddenly, the race is on. Like troops storming a beach, cavalcades of | 341
workers surge into the streets to take refuge in the subways where, ex- | 356
hausted after a hard day's work, only the most agile find seats. The | 370
others stand, many striving to maintain their balance by hanging onto the | 384
swaying straps overhead or onto the metal handles of nearby seats. | 398

There seems to be little or no break as a new panorama unfolds. The | 412
night people swarm into the streets--pressing, pushing, and rushing to | 426
various places of entertainment. Once again there is the click of heels, | 441
the shuffling of feet, the flashing of jewel-like lights inviting the pass- | 456
erby to places of entertainment. On the surface the city has become a | 470
fascinating world of glamour and luxury, but underneath, that view may be | 484
as unreal as a snow scene contained in a glass bubble. | 496

| 1 | 2 | 3 | 4 | 5 | 6 | 7 | 8 | 9 | 10 | 11 | 12 | 13 | 14 | 15

Drill 2 (Each line contains 63 strokes.)

The development of our community would fail without management.
A satisfied customer is another valuable asset of our new firm.
Your personal habits will seldom be very interesting to others.
Whatever originates at the gathering may vindicate our beliefs.
Important achievement is possible if tremendous effort is made.

Drill 3 (Each line contains 65 strokes.)

Everyone questioned antisocial behavior and found it undesirable.
A dynamic, economical program of the institution is an advantage.
He is an ardent individual and a very qualified attention getter.
The youngster's predilection for mischief tempers our generosity.
Amiable customers eliminate problems confronting many businesses.

Drill 4 (Each line contains 66 strokes.)

A famous woman furnished them with somewhat practical information.
The element of competition constitutes a serious spending problem.
A combination of amusing anecdotes provided the proper atmosphere.
The influential instructor contemplated a flexible typing program.
It is somewhat comforting to achieve fantastic progress in typing.

Drill 5 (Each line contains 68 strokes.)

Hostile conditions on the peninsula dissuaded us from the adventure.
The intelligent deployment of strategic weaponry is a major concern.
You must endeavor to determine your chosen fields of specialization.
Separating families encourages the destruction of family solidarity.
Modern methods are available so you can achieve tremendous progress.

Drill 6 (Each line contains 70 strokes.)

You will eventually comprehend how you developed your speed in typing.
Your vivid imagination makes an important contribution to the picture.
A naturalist was particularly concerned about substantial differences.
A sojourn on the highway provided us a pleasant respite from drudgery.
An improvement in clerical skills represents a helpful accomplishment.

TIMED WRITING 11

Everyone's life is measured by time--minutes, hours, and years. A   13
giant clock in one of our largest cities has one hand that extends almost   28
six yards and weighs a ton, and although this hand moves twenty yards each   43
hour, its movement is barely visible. Symbolically, the movement of the   58
hands on a clock should remind us that wasted minutes and hours are lost   73
forever; they can never be retrieved.   80

Yesterday is history--tomorrow may never come. Today--actually, only   94
this moment--belongs to you. You are the product today of how wisely you   109
used the minutes, hours, and days that are past. Your success tomorrow   124
will be the direct result of how you utilize your time today. Your whole   138
future depends upon overcoming problems and surmounting barriers that may   153
hinder your progress. By using every hour effectively, you steadily move   168
toward a satisfactory work situation and increase your efficiency.   182

If you consciously direct your efforts toward achieving a desired end,   196
you are sure to succeed. Without a goal, there can be no struggle; without   211
struggle, there can be no victory. You must devise a specific plan or goal   226
and work toward it. Until this plan is formulated, you have nothing to   241
reach for and no way of knowing when you have achieved your goal.   254

Everyone likes action, yet some become lethargic and time wasters the   268
moment they arrive at their place of work. This deficiency cannot be over-   283
come unless you discipline yourself aggressively. You stand in the midst   298
of fundamental choices. Reason does not work automatically nor is thinking   313
a mechanical process. Of your own volition, you must set your standards   328
and your code of values and work toward living up to them. There is no   342
surer way to destroy your creative instincts than to stifle or ignore them.   357

If you allow yourself to settle for less than your full ability,   371
decay sets in. Your mind is the driver of your fingers, and you must drive   386
as far as your mind will take you, with excellence as your goal. Individ-   401
uals who coast downhill are at the mercy of unknown elements. Through   415
sacrifice of leisure time and hard work, you will succeed in excelling in   430
typing, and pride will be part of your reward.   439

Every act of your life has to be willed. Thus you can rise as far in   453
typing skills as you are willing, but you must pay for this in time and   467
energy. The choice is yours to make. The choice should be the dedication   482
of yourself to your highest potential of excellence. As you progress, you   497
will feel the personal satisfaction that everyone feels after doing a job   512
well.   513

| 1 | 2 | 3 | 4 | 5 | 6 | 7 | 8 | 9 | 10 | 11 | 12 | 13 | 14 | 15 |

Drill 9 (Each line contains 74 strokes.)

Do we wish to go to the hot jail to find a man who is now out of his mind?

Do all the good you can to all the people you can in every manner you can.

If they work hard at their typing, they should be very good at their work.

Whether or not we wish to turn down the option is something to be decided.

An extra practice period each day will help you improve your typing speed.

Drill 10 (Each line contains 75 strokes.)

It is time for the boy and man to fish in the stream to catch their dinner.

You will be a good typist if you will follow the paths of typing champions.

It is better to have tried typing once and failed than never to have tried.

Do your best in typing daily and you will be very pleased with the results.

After doing these drills, your typing rate should be tremendously improved.

SPEED STUDY 2
HIGH-STROKE-INTENSITY SENTENCES

Purpose: To develop fluency in typing long words.

Features: Each sentence contains a large number of long words. These sentences are arranged so that those with the least number of long words precede those that have a heavier concentration of them in each drill.

Line: 75 spaces

Drill Assignment: For Diagnostic Test 1, use Drills 1 and 6; for Diagnostic Test 2, use Drills 2 and 7; for Diagnostic Test 3, use Drills 3 and 8; for Diagnostic Test 4, use Drills 4 and 9; for Diagnostic Test 5, use Drills 5 and 10.

Directions: Type each line perfectly ten times—not necessarily in succession, but in total—and double-space between groups of ten perfect lines. Start typing each sentence slowly, and gradually increase your typing rate as your fingers get accustomed to the sentence.

Drill 1 (Each line contains 61 strokes.)

Their personality and proficiency contributed to their cause.

There is a tendency for our pursuits to thwart our ambitions.

During my college days everything was completely fascinating.

A mysterious element yielded a surprisingly visible vitality.

Something obviously affected their expert financial judgment.

Words

Individuals perceive their work situations in numerous ways. Some   13
perceive their work as drudgery, as the only means available to pay the   28
rent and to buy food and other essentials. Others perceive work as a   42
source of power over others, while others perceive work as an outlet for   56
creativity. Yet, in each case, as the perceived need is met, higher-level   71
needs emerge and influence the behavior of the individual.   83

Your work will be either satisfying or frustrating, depending upon   97
your ability to function capably with other people and in a variety of   111
situations. A certain amount of frustration, anxiety, self-doubt, or in-   126
difference may be expected to accrue as you perform any task. But these   140
need not give you a feeling of inadequacy. In fact, as you recognize these   155
symptoms, you should feel challenged to fulfill the requirements of each   170
assignment.   173

Do not expect everything in a work situation to be perfect. Most   186
people are responsible and dependable, and they put in a fair amount of   200
effort for their wages. Of course, there are exceptions; and the trouble-   215
makers 'and chronic complainers are always more conspicuous than hardwork-   230
ing, honest individuals.   235

In the competitive climate in which we live, more than anything else   249
you will need to use your typing talent to the utmost, act independently   263
whenever possible, and prove your capability in this skill. Analyze and   278
evaluate your potential capabilities and typing skill. Apply all your re-   293
sources to improving the development and use of this talent. Good plan-   307
ning, work organization, and a respect for deadlines will win you the   321
gratitude of your supervisor and of his or her superiors.   333

You should perceive the goals of the organization as being relevant to   347
your personal objectives. You not only serve your organization, you repre-   362
sent your organization and your supervisor. This fact imposes serious   376
responsibilities upon you as a person and as a typist. Everything you type   391
should be as nearly perfect as possible. Occasionally, a part of your work   407
may seem to be unimportant. This work may not be important to you, but to   422
a keen observer, it may have unusual significance. Always remember that   436
your typing provides someone with a permanent record of the important   450
decisions and functions of your organization.   460

A renowned artist once said that trifles make perfection, but perfec-   473
tion is no trifle. This statement is as applicable to typing as it is to   488
art. You must constantly strive for excellence in order to become a pro-   503
ficient typist.   506

| 1 | 2 | 3 | 4 | 5 | 6 | 7 | 8 | 9 | 10 | 11 | 12 | 13 | 14 | 15

Drill 4 (Each line contains 69 strokes.)

Now and then it is true that we can do very well if we want to do so.
This is the time for men and women to come to the aid of their party.
If your ship sails due north, it will come near the top of the world.
A good personality will make it easier for them to make good friends.
To make the best progress, therefore, do your best work at all times.

Drill 5 (Each line contains 69 strokes.)

See if I can go and help them to do a fine job for the men and women.
Now is a fine time to do some of the great things you may want to do.
You should give your employers the best you have or seek another job.
It is a fact that the faster you type the more you will like to type.
There are some folks who will go to the south to find what they want.

Drill 6 (Each line contains 71 strokes.)

Is it for the lack of faith and work that we fail in a task hard to do?
I am sorry that you are not sure of the two women who came to our home.
His day has come and so will yours if you try to do your best each day.
He and they should go to their jobs today if it does not rain too much.
She may not put the effort into typing that she must do to become fast.

Drill 7 (Each line contains 72 strokes.)

On a hot day the girl went for a walk to see the big rocks with her dad.
The ten men ran down the lane, and it is up to the judges as to who won.
It will be a fine thing if we do what is paid for or refund their money.
During our time of need, we may go to our friends for help and sympathy.
One thing is certain--good practice will produce good results in typing.

Drill 8 (Each line contains 73 strokes.)

It is a fact that more and more fine jobs will go to the fastest typists.
Knowing what to type and how to type is the fastest way to make progress.
It is the souls of men and women which permit them to rise above animals.
One can endure many trials, but the lack of progress is one of the worst.
Try to strike your keys in a steady, timely fashion without undue pauses.

	Words
Quality, not quantity, should be the first objective in any type of	14
work. The aspect of productivity that is easy to forget is that quantity	28
without quality is valueless. Progress and success are affected to a great	44
extent by how one performs small duties. Often it is the little details	58
that form the bone and sinew of great successes. If you can be relied upon	73
to carry out small assignments carefully and accurately, you will generally	89
be relied upon to perform the greater ones. Nothing shows your character	103
as clearly as the way you do small things. If these are done in a slipshod	119
manner, no one will trust you to do the complicated, troublesome tasks.	133
The quality of your work will mark you for success or failure.	146
Sometimes one is tempted to rush through a task in a desire to save	160
time. This is a mistake. You must stay in control of every situation.	174
Rushing not only wastes time and energy but inflicts the needless burden of	189
typing many pages again and again that could have been typed perfectly the	204
first time. If you follow this lazy procedure, you are cheating yourself.	220
We all live in the midst of distractions. During almost every waking	234
moment, we are besieged by bids for our attention. Certain thoughts, memo-	249
ries, feelings, and worries are always ready to intrude. We cannot	263
avoid them, but we can make a determined effort to shut out unrelated mes-	278
sages that tend to distract our attention from work. To accomplish this,	293
we must concentrate on producing a quality product each time we perform an	308
assignment, whether it is a routine task or one that requires total	321
concentration.	324
It is unnecessary to allow poor quality work to handicap one through-	338
out life. Everyone has personal assets and talents that have never been	353
realized. Talent is an innate ability, but skills are learned. Typing is	368
considered a production skill, and you alone set your level of accomplish-	383
ment. Never be content with partially learning typing techniques, for you	398
quickly forget what has been barely learned. The chief value of your typ-	412
ing knowledge and skill is the practical use that you make of them.	426
Furthermore, your typing skill is closely related to other aspects of your	441
life by helping you to do your work more efficiently and to live a happier	456
and more comfortable life.	462
Your ability to type rapidly and accurately gives you a personal	475
advantage that can contribute to your position, your self-confidence and,	490
of course, your career. Quality is your key to success.	501

| 1 | 2 | 3 | 4 | 5 | 6 | 7 | 8 | 9 | 10 | 11 | 12 | 13 | 14 | 15 |

SPEED STUDY 1
SIMPLE-VOCABULARY SENTENCES

Purpose: To develop fluency in typing common, simple words.

Features: These sentences contain a concentration of the 200 most commonly used words in the English language.

Line: 75 spaces

Drill Assignment: For Diagnostic Test 1, use Drills 1 and 6; for Diagnostic Test 2, use Drills 2 and 7; for Diagnostic Test 3, use Drills 3 and 8; for Diagnostic Test 4, use Drills 4 and 9; for Diagnostic Test 5, use Drills 5 and 10.

Directions: Type each line perfectly ten times. Begin at a slow rate of speed, and gradually increase your typing rate until you are typing at a fast, accurate rate of speed. If you make an error in typing a line, return your carriage/carrier immediately and begin a new line. You should have ten perfect lines—not necessarily in succession, but in total—before you double-space and begin the next line. Always double-space between groups of ten perfect lines.

Drill 1   (Each line contains 65 strokes.)

You must force yourself to type fast, so make an effort to do so.

It is up to you and me to find out if he is to go to the pit now.

Our boy is to go to the file and do some work on it at this time.

Six men will come to the aid of the boys and girls of this store.

More and more men and women will vote this year in the elections.

Drill 2   (Each line contains 66 strokes.)

If we like to type, we will do it as well as it is in us to do so.

It is not what you do, but the way you do it that counts the most.

If the fox can run faster than the dog, it will get away this day.

Now it is up to you to type fast and without errors when you type.

To see a champion typist at work is like viewing poetry in motion.

Drill 3   (Each line contains 67 strokes.)

In a day or two I may turn down the quiet man from the nearby city.

The past day is one we will find more and more to our satisfaction.

Typing a simple sentence, many times, is a good way to build speed.

It does not matter whether you type fast or slow; type with rhythm.

You will improve your typing if you will practice the right things.

TIMED WRITING 14

A positive attitude is one of the greatest assets. Guard it care- | 13
fully. Progress and success, whether in the classroom, on the job, or at | 28
home, are affected to a great extent by it. Your personality also reveals | 43
your readiness to assume the responsibilities involved in a job or in | 57
social contacts. | 61

Examine your inner self critically to ensure that no negative tenden- | 74
cies intrude. If you have a martyr complex and foster feelings of inferi- | 89
ority or if you make excuses for poor work or for too little done, you are | 104
rationalizing deficiencies. Other negative traits that drain you of vital- | 119
ity, rob you of efficiency, and dull your brain power are depression, | 133
tension, irritation, and intolerance. Your attitude toward your fellow | 148
classmates or workers, toward supervision, and toward responsibility is as | 163
important as your attitude about yourself. | 171

Psychologists tell us that attitude is an enduring structure of be- | 185
liefs that causes us to behave selectively toward physical objects, events, | 200
and behavior. Thus we conclude that a positive mental concept of our | 214
ability and worth is extremely important in striving toward a goal. Con- | 229
versely, it is impossible to progress satisfactorily in work or live a | 243
meaningful life if one is filled with negative perceptions. | 255

Perception of yourself is a powerful force that influences and guides | 269
you. If you perceive yourself as becoming a successful typist, you will | 283
see yourself as responsible for your progress and you will pinpoint what | 298
you do, or fail to do, that causes your success or failure. You will rein- | 313
force your attainments and correct your errors. You know that you guide | 327
your destiny in typing; and since you perceive that you are competent, you | 342
will invest your time, energy, and talents in full measure today so you may | 358
reap the benefits of a superior typing skill tomorrow. | 369

Typing is one of the most important ways of conveying information. | 382
You, the typist, will be judged by the quality of the product produced, and | 397
your attitude will be displayed by your work. | 407

Two of the most important aspects of a positive attitude are interest | 421
and desire. If you are interested, you will absorb more information from | 436
your surroundings, and you will become aware of opportunities that further | 451
your goal. Desire will make you more creative. These attitudes make you | 466
search for new opportunities and new approaches to implement ideas. A | 480
person with a positive attitude reflects a sense of accomplishment. | 493

| 1 | 2 | 3 | 4 | 5 | 6 | 7 | 8 | 9 | 10 | 11 | 12 | 13 | 14 | 15

SECTION 7

SPEED
STUDIES

Simple-Vocabulary Sentences	90	Double-Letter Sentences	98
High-Stroke-Intensity Sentences	92	One-Hand-Word Sentences	100
Alternate-Hand Sentences	94	Alphabetic Sentences	101
Compound- and Multiple-Stroke Sentences	96	Frequent-Spacing Sentences	103
Vertical-Stroke Sentences	97	Frequent-Shifting Sentences	104

Words

A great deal has been written about champions in many fields, but — 13
little has been written about champion typists. Since this book is about — 28
championship typing techniques and methods, the characteristics found in — 43
the rarest of all champions, the champion typist, will be considered. — 57

It is an electrifying, motivating experience to watch a champion's — 70
fingers flying over the typewriter keys at more than one hundred and sixty — 85
words a minute without making a single error. There is nothing more dra- — 100
matic to a student than to observe a champion typist in action. — 113

Champion typists are made; they are not born. However, there are some — 127
indispensable qualities inherent in a champion that distinguishes that — 141
individual from ordinary typists. There is a subtle combination of abil- — 156
ity, perception, perseverance, and dedication within the individual that is — 171
augmented by the long, sometimes frustrating, and often tedious hours, — 186
weeks, and even years of practice needed to reach the final goal. — 199

The champion soon learns that technique is the major concern. What — 212
may appear insignificant to an ordinary typist is of paramount importance — 227
to a champion. The height of the chair or desk is a tremendous factor, — 242
since one inch can make the difference of at least ten net words a minute. — 257
A quick, firm striking of the keys is essential for speed. Fingers should — 272
never linger on the keys, and fingers must be curved and hover closely to — 287
the keyboard. Incorrect stroking will result in errors and loss of speed. — 302

So many different reaches are involved in typing that one must master — 316
each one of them to avoid jerky motions or unnecessary pauses and to — 330
develop smoothness and continuity in stroking. — 339

Just as champions learned from laborious practice, you, too, must — 352
first learn how to work with your machine if you wish to develop superior — 367
typing skills. Striking the keys correctly is a technique which must be — 382
developed before you can reach a high level of speed and accuracy. There — 397
are several important areas you should emphasize: position of the fingers, — 412
wrists, forearms, and elbows; touch; rhythm; and total concentration. — 426

Although you may spend your working day with fingers flying over a — 440
keyboard, there are probably some mistakes you continue to make. These — 454
problems must be attacked separately by analyzing each area and practic- — 469
ing until the difficulty is eliminated. There is no substitute for proper — 483
practice methods and techniques, so learn the championship way and start — 498
on the road to high-speed typing. — 504

| 1 | 2 | 3 | 4 | 5 | 6 | 7 | 8 | 9 | 10 | 11 | 12 | 13 | 14 | 15 |

Drill 12

Antitrust enforcement is premised on the concept that self-regulating forces of competition are preferred to either government regulation, on the one hand, or private utilization of economic power, on the other hand, to gain control over, or to apply anticompetitive strictures within, competitive markets. Therefore, antitrust targets trade practices falling within the latter category.

Drill 13

Simple regression analysis of average costs versus demand for general aviation services has the advantage of avoiding potential distortion of parameter values caused by multicollinearity in a multivariate analysis. But there is the disadvantage of using a partial model in which a substantial amount of variation in use response remains unaccounted for, due primarily to differences in real disposable income levels of consumers and the amount of alternative substitutable services selected.

Drill 14

As the complexity of administering a municipal organization involved in providing a multiplicity of diverse human and physical services grows, the need for an efficient delivery structure to optimize the utilization of limited resources becomes more acute. Implementation of modern management techniques and development of an integrated information system and program generation capability which will derive maximum effective usage of appropriate electronic data processing equipment appear to be viable methods to facilitate program implementation and administration. Such refinement is necessary for a city with a slow anticipated revenue base growth.

Drill 15

In this participatory-collaborative process, two important things do happen. First, with regard to particular aspects of planning, synthesis of differing views leads to a consensus--a result which often does not correspond to anyone's initial view. Second, reiteration of similar insights by many sources gives special credence to the general validity and applicability of the concept. In short, as concrete steps have been taken to implement effective planning for the statistical system, the planning process itself has evolved in ways that no one could foresee at the beginning.

SECTION 4

DIAGNOSTIC TESTS

Purpose: To diagnose individual weaknesses in speed or accuracy.

Features: Each sentence emphasizes one particular type of problem area. The sentence number corresponds to the drill number of the appropriate corrective practice. For example, the appropriate corrective practice for Diagnostic Test 1, sentence 3, is Accuracy Study 3, Drill 1, if accuracy is the problem or Speed Study 3, Drill 1, if speed is the problem.

Line: 70 spaces

Directions: Take a 1-minute timing on each of the ten specially constructed sentences. Record your correct words a minute (CWAM) and error scores for each 1-minute timing in the appropriate spaces in the Pretest columns for the diagnostic tests indicated on Chart 3: Speed and Accuracy Analysis. Then follow either the speed or accuracy routine as outlined in the directions for Chart 3. After you complete the appropriate corrective drills, take a second set of 1-minute timings on each sentence in the same diagnostic test and record your scores in the Posttest column on Chart 3. This will enable you to determine how much improvement you have made in speed and accuracy.

Drill 7

These international logistics requirements have been developed from within a broad array of options made possible from the fluid constraints provided by your letter and within the variety of thresholds that have been developed from an array of interpretations of these constraints. In order to add some semblance of substance to allow for solidified requirements to be developed, we have arbitrarily established comprehensive collection of thresholds.

Drill 8

This is to certify that, to the best of my knowledge and belief, the cumulative total of man-hours expended by labor category from contract outset to the end of the term contemplated by the term effort of the contract schedule and in support of the work called for by said term effort of the contract schedule as set forth in this report is accurate and complete.

Drill 9

Authority redelegated herein to a position by title may be exercised by a person officially designated to serve in such position in an acting capacity or on a temporary basis, unless prohibited by a restriction placed into the document designating him or her as "acting" or unless not legally permissible.

Drill 10

A board whose membership is composed of personnel from the command activity whose function is to systematically evaluate, coordinate, recommend approval or disapproval, and implement approved changes in configuration of a configuration item after formal establishment of its configuration identification will enhance our overall effectiveness.

Drill 11

In a world of conflicting and perhaps pathogenic expectations as to what are adequate levels of security, it is becoming increasingly apparent that greater effort must be directed to the formidable task of distinguishing cognitions of national security threat from identifiable trends and conditions associated with specific threat stimuli.

DIAGNOSTIC TEST 1

1 See if we can go and help them to do a fine job for the men and women.
2 Hostile conditions on the peninsula dissuaded them from the adventure.
3 Their neurotic visitor may burn down the five docks if he is not paid.
4 The pure vein of our silver was more than we had anticipated at first.
5 My annual bazaar grew swiftly and dazzled many overburdened lobbyists.
6 The bookkeeping committee from Tennessee embarrassed a football coach.
7 My nylon dress was the best garb she could wear to the bazaar at noon.
8 A quick movement of the bold enemy will jeopardize six good divisions.
9 I am to see if I am to do it now or if he is to do it at a later time.
10 It Is The Duty Of A King To Do Me A Turn If He Can And He Is To Do So.
    | 1 | 2 | 3 | 4 | 5 | 6 | 7 | 8 | 9 | 10 | 11 | 12 | 13 | 14

DIAGNOSTIC TEST 2

1 This is a fine time to do some of the great things you may wish to do.
2 An improvement in clerical skills represents a helpful accomplishment.
3 Your ancient ivory emblem is an ornament to enrich and endow the city.
4 Whether they find more stores can make a big change in our selections.
5 A cold swan swiftly swam my brook and decided to dazzle its own flock.
6 An appellee cheerfully accommodated the aggressive coffee connoisseur.
7 The dazed bears raged in their cages as a lion slyly looked on nearby.
8 Extra work on psychology enabled five juniors to pass your major quiz.
9 It is the job of the aide to help me if he can and he is to do it now.
10 See If We Can Go With Them And Also Help To Do A Fine Job For The Men.
    | 1 | 2 | 3 | 4 | 5 | 6 | 7 | 8 | 9 | 10 | 11 | 12 | 13 | 14

DIAGNOSTIC TEST 3

1 Now is the time for men and women to come to the aid of their country.
2 A sojourn on the highway provided us a pleasant respite from drudgery.
3 The authenticity of the proxy vote did torment the lame duck official.
4 Your piano will last as long as the quiet lady plays it in a fine way.
5 My umbrella survived a heartbreaking blizzard and innumerable hazards.
6 The committee from Mississippi suppressed a report from my bookkeeper.
7 Our ill-fed polo pony only stared at a puny onion in his filthy stall.
8 The quiet preacher's texts just amazed forty very willing backsliders.
9 If it is up to me to do it, I am not for it at this or any other time.
10 Now And Then It Is True That We Can Do More Than We Thought If We Try.
    | 1 | 2 | 3 | 4 | 5 | 6 | 7 | 8 | 9 | 10 | 11 | 12 | 13 | 14

Drill 3

The unprecedented nature of this action is fully recognized. Nevertheless, it is offered in a sincere effort to illuminate a classic example of the distinctive contrariety and dysfunctional qualities of deep-seated personal biases and institutionalized racism when they are allowed to permeate the administrative and operational fiber of any organization.

Drill 4

The purpose is to evaluate the complexities involved in dealing with interdependent parent-and-child outcome dimensions, as well as with the complexities of longitudinal relationships between early and long-run developmental effects on mothers, target infants, siblings, and other family members to provide critical evidence of retained and multiplier effects.

Drill 5

The convenience of multiple wall clocks depicting the actual time in different time zones throughout the world outweighs the minuscule savings advanced by the attached suggestion. The plethora of required signs in military air terminals is relieved by the additional clocks, not only because of their pictorial value but also because of their contribution to the esthetics of the facility.

Drill 6

In addition to an overview of the organization and management concepts and theory applicable to all types of administrative units, the attachment incorporates a brief analysis of the evolution of management functions and practices in representative contexts. Periodic assessments, from a systems viewpoint, of ethical and moral issues confronting personnel functioning in an extraordinarily complex contemporary sociotechnical environment are very clearly of utmost imperativeness.

DIAGNOSTIC TEST 4

1   Six men will come to the aid of the boys and girls of this fine store.

2   A naturalist was particularly concerned about substantial differences.

3   The proficiency of our neighbors did enchant and enrich their auditor.

4   I might take the option on the house if proper financing can be found.

5   The eccentric recluse decided to deduct innumerable gifts from my kin.

6   A buzzard effectively puzzled and dazzled the bobbing, hopping rabbit.

7   A puny puppy chased a fat, crazed cat in the grass area of the crater.

8   Zinnias, meekly vying for a bright effect, juxtaposed yellow jonquils.

9   See if it is to be done now or if we can do it all in the near future.

10 It Is I Who Will Have To Do Some Of The Things That I Will Not Do Now.
    | 1 | 2 | 3 | 4 | 5 | 6 | 7 | 8 | 9 | 10 | 11 | 12 | 13 | 14

DIAGNOSTIC TEST 5

1   It is not what you do, but the way you do it that now counts the most.

2   Their combination of amusing anecdotes provided the proper atmosphere.

3   The dormant social problems did dismay our busy neighbor on the right.

4   There might be more jobs for everyone in the county if we plan for it.

5   Many hungry humans succeeded in surviving the unusually frigid autumn.

6   A pretty puppy appears to chase a raccoon into the hills successfully.

7   Your ill pupil fell into an oily pool as he dared to walk on its edge.

8   The quaint enzyme puzzled several exceptional judges before weakening.

9   A king is to do me a turn if he can as it is his sacred duty to do so.

10 It Is Up To You And Them To Find Out If Mary Is To Go To The Play Now.
    | 1 | 2 | 3 | 4 | 5 | 6 | 7 | 8 | 9 | 10 | 11 | 12 | 13 | 14

Drill 5

in nothing flat in nothing flat in nothing flat in nothing flat in nothing

the quick kill the quick kill the quick kill the quick kill the quick kill

they saw women they saw women they saw women they saw women they saw women

and that thing and that thing and that thing and that thing and that thing

ACCURACY STUDY 29
CONCENTRATION DRILLS—PARAGRAPHS

Purpose: To enhance accuracy by improving concentration.

Features: These drills contain a great deal of bureaucratic language, especially the type found in government publications and correspondence.

Line: 75 spaces

Directions: Type each paragraph on a line-for-line basis, and type each line perfectly two times. That is, type the first line perfectly twice. Then type the second line perfectly twice, and so on. In typing each line perfectly two times, you do not have to type the lines perfectly consecutively, but in total. Do not attempt to edit or comprehend what you are typing but, rather, concentrate on typing each word perfectly. You are to spell out each word that you type—letter for letter—and endeavor to maintain perfect rhythm in typing this assignment. Type all 15 drills.

Drill 1

It is thought to be methodologically innovative in its use of economic
input-output techniques integrated with detailed industry-centered, as well
as weapon-system-centered, studies to gauge the likely impact of sharp in-
creases or decreases in defense procurement on the U.S. industrial system.

Drill 2

The absence of fully programming those enlisted manpower requirements
without a concomitant reduction in either ship capability requirements or
endurance parameters forms a dichotomy between our stated mission-objective
and the individual unit's ability to carry out the specified mission in a
peacetime environment.

SECTION 5

SKILL-DEVELOPMENT PARAGRAPHS

Purpose: To develop speed and accuracy in typing ordinary paragraphs for a period of 1 minute.

Features: These paragraphs contain a large number of common words, with a balanced concentration of various stroke combinations. Each succeeding paragraph is increased in length by 5 words, thereby requiring greater speed with perfect accuracy.

Line: 75 spaces

Directions: Type each paragraph within 1 minute without making a single error, beginning with the 20-word paragraph and progressing as far as you can. Type each paragraph on a line-for-line basis.

ACCURACY STUDY 28
CONCENTRATION DRILLS—SPLIT DOUBLETS

Purpose: To increase accuracy by improving concentration, thereby facilitating the typing of split doublets (in which one word ends and the next word begins with the same letter).

Features: These drills consist of phrases containing split doublets, which constitute a major typing problem to anyone typing at a high rate of speed. These drills will require a high degree of concentration in order to avoid omitting the second half of the doublet.

Line: 75 spaces

Directions: Type each line perfectly five times—not necessarily in succession, but in total. In order to type split doublets accurately, it may be necessary for you to spell out each letter. You should begin typing each line slowly and gradually increase your typing rate as you become accustomed to typing split doublets.

Drill 1

the civic center the civic center the civic center the civic center
and the red dogs and the red dogs and the red dogs and the red dogs
and the big gate and the big gate and the big gate and the big gate
and high-handed and high-handed and high-handed and high-handed and

Drill 2

and on notice and on notice and on notice and on notice and on notice
and the error and the error and the error and the error and the error
left or right left or right left or right left or right left or right
and jab badly and jab badly and jab badly and jab badly and jab badly

Drill 3

and is sure and is sure and is sure and is sure and is sure and is sure
and top pay and top pay and top pay and top pay and top pay and top pay
and after reading and after reading and after reading and after reading
and will look kindly and will look kindly and will look kindly and will

Drill 4

know why and know why and know why and know why and know why and know why
so often and so often and so often and so often and so often and so often
my youth and my youth and my youth and my youth and my youth and my youth
if found and if found and if found and if found and if found and if found

20 WORDS

Knowing what to type as well as how to type will make it possible for you to become a very good typist.

25 WORDS

If you are energetic and if you will follow instructions, you will enjoy typing. You will also acquire a very important skill.

30 WORDS

Typing can be fun. All you have to do is concentrate on developing championship typing techniques, and if you succeed, you will really love to type.

35 WORDS

You have learned the location of the keys on the typewriter. Your future progress will depend upon your practicing the right drills in the right way. Type as you have been told.

40 WORDS

Students who put forth their best effort in learning to type find that they do much better than other students. Therefore, give typing the very best you have, and the very best will come back to you.

45 WORDS

No matter what your goal in typing is, there is one fact you must realize: a typewriter will reflect only the energy and desire you put into it. If you will not do anything, the typewriter will do the same, so do your best.

Drill 4

ynam nees evah I ,moorssalc gnipyt eht ni neeb evah I sraey eht revO
ti ,sesac emos ni ,dna ylreporp gnitartnecnoc ytluciffid dah ohw stneduts
yreve ni ,revewoH .laicifeneb ton saw sdrawkcab gnipyt taht deraeppa sah
yletelpmoc gnitartnecnoc smelborp dah ohw stneduts eht fo lla ,ssalc elgnis
-kcab gnipyt yb devloser ylirotcafsitas melborp eht dah gnipyt rieht no
;sdrawkcab sllird wef a gnipyt deriuqer ylno ti ,secnatsni emos nI .sdraw
;sdrawkcab depyt eb ot dah sllird fo tes eritne eht ,sesac emos ni elihw
.semit eerht ro owt sllird fo tes eritne eht epyt ot dah srehto wef a dna
-woh ;yrogetac hcae otni llaf lliw ohw enimretederp ot elbissop ton si tI
ot tnemngissa siht fo sgnipyt eerht ro ,owt ,eno sekat ti rehtehw ,reve
latnem yrassecen eht deriuqca evah uoy taht si gniht tnatropmi eht ,eciffus
.ti htrow eb ylniatrec lliw tI .tsipyt etarucca na emoceb ot enilpicsid

Drill 5

eht epyt ot evah lliw ohw stneduts eht fo eno eb ot neppah uoy fI
elbuod uoy taht tseggus dluow I ,ecno naht erom tnemngissa sdrawkcab gnipyt
,sdrow rehto nI .epyt lliw uoy taht hcae fo senil tcefrep fo rebmun eht
senil tcefrep owt epyt ot dah uoy ,tnemngissa siht depyt uoy emit tsrif eht
fo rebmun eht elbuod ,tnemngissa siht epyt uoy emit dnoces ehT .hcae fo
-nigeb ,hcae fo senil tcefrep ruof epyt lliw uoy os ,hcae fo senil tcefrep
dah evah I .yrassecen fi ,62 ydutS hguorht epyt dna 32 ydutS htiw gnin
driht a tnemngissa eht epyt ot dah ohw dnasuoht net fo tuo tneduts eno ylno
setunim evif epyt ot elba saw ehs ,ti gnipyt detelpmoc ehs nehw ,dna ,emit
-woh ,emit taht ot roirP .rorre eno naht erom on htiw ypoc thgiarts morf
.gnimit etunim-evif a no srorre ytriht ot neetfif morf ekam dluow ehs ,reve
.gnipyt ni noitartnecnoc latot fo ecnatropmi eht setacidni ylraelc sihT

50 WORDS

To type accurately, you must develop the habit of analyzing each error, recording each on your error-analysis chart, and exercising care not to make that error again. If you will follow the corrective measures outlined, you will type more accurately.

55 WORDS

One of the important questions you have to answer right now is whether you will expend the energy it takes to master typing. You are following the trail of champions, and you will save yourself a great deal of frustration by conscientiously doing what you are instructed.

60 WORDS

One of the proudest moments in my life was the first time I was able to type sixty words in a minute without making any errors. You are at the brink of discovering this marvelous feeling. In order to accomplish this feat, you must type at the rate of five strokes a second without making any errors.

65 WORDS

It is a fascinating thing to observe one who is able to type fast and accurately. It means that this individual has spent time mastering the right way to do all of the operations in typing and has also followed a carefully designed skill-development program to develop superior typing skills. That is what you are doing now.

70 WORDS

You cannot become proficient in typing unless you have a positive attitude. Therefore, each time you sit at your typewriter you should believe that you are going to do some wonderful typing today. If you really believe in yourself, you will find that you will type rapidly and accurately, so have confidence in yourself and you will progress steadily.

Drill 1

gniriuqca si gnitirwepyt fo lla ni smelborp tluciffid tsom eht fo enO

slaudividni weF   .tsipyt etarucca yrev a emoceb ot enilpicsid latnem eht

ot deriuqer noitartnecnoc etulosba dna latot eht fo noitpecnoc yna evah

poleved tsum uoy taht uoy erussa em teL   .yletarucca ylbanosaer epyt

-ni emos nI   .yletarucca epyt ot redro ni srewop evitartnecnoc suodnemert

sdrawkcab tnemngissa na epyt ot tneduts a rof yrassecen si ti ,secnats

si sihT   .gnipyt reh ro sih no etartnecnoc ot elba si tneduts eht erofeb

.tnasaelp oot ton si ti ,wonk I ,dna tnemom siht ta gniod era uoy tahw

I ,gnipyt fo esahp siht retsam ot evirts ot eunitnoc ylno lliw uoy fi ,teY

.eveihca lliw uoy stluser eht htiw desaelp yrev eb lliw uoy wonk

Drill 2

I--oga sraey ytriht naht erom--gnipyt gnihcaet nageb tsrif I nehW

-of ytluciffid fo laed taerg a dah ohw stneduts fo rebmun a deretnuocne

rehtie dluow yehT   .gnipyt erew yeht tahw no noitnetta eritne rieht gnisuc

kniht dluow yeht ro gnipyt erew yeht tahw fo txetnoc eht ni detseretni teg

-ert a edam stneduts ynam ,ecneuqesnoc a sA   .rettam suoenartxe emos tuoba

gnittimo ,srettel gnidda sa hcus ,srorre noitartnecnoc fo rebmun suodnem

ylraelc sihT   .srettel gnorw eht gnilbuod ro ,srettel gnisopsnart ,srettel

enilpicsid latnem reporp eht depoleved ton dah yeht taht em ot detacidni

-inam noitartnecnoc fo kcal eht yb delbuort os saw I   .yletarucca epyt ot

.detnemelpmi eb ot dah serusaem citsard emos wenk I taht detsef

Drill 3

.stluser derised eht eveihca dluow taht od dluoc I tahw derednow I

.eulb eht fo tuo tlob a ekil em ot emac ti ekawa-flah yal I sa thgin enO

-pyt rieht no yletelpmoc etartnecnoc stneduts ym ekam ot yaw tseb ehT

,esruoc fo ,tnaem sihT   .sdrawkcab epyt yeht taht eriuqer ot eb dluow gni

.ylgnidrocca epyt dna tfel ot thgir morf daer ot dah stneduts eht taht

a teg ton did I taht yrros erew yeht em dlot stneduts ynam ,emit taht tA

ot hcaorppa levon siht gnizilautpecnoc fo daetsni ,peels s'thgin lluf

sraey ytriht naht erom ,yadoT   .srorre noitartnecnoc rieht gniyfitcer

gnitcerroc ot troser lanif a sa sdrawkcab gnipyt gnisu llits ma I ,retal

.tneduts elgnis yreve no gnikrow llits si ti dna ,srorre noitartnecnoc

75 WORDS

You must maintain a steady tempo in typing in order to type fast. I have seen many people type rapidly in spurts only to lose the speed advantage made in the spurt by a long pause--during which the typist endeavors to line the fingers in position to type the next word. A pause robs you of speed, so do not pause. Keep your carriage or carrier moving without any hesitation.

80 WORDS

Success in typewriting is usually the result of doing the right thing, in the right way, with zest and regularity. This is why it is vitally important that you type a certain way. The importance of good typing habits cannot be overemphasized. Each drill in this book has been carefully and scientifically planned to provide you with a systematic development of typing skills to guarantee success.

85 WORDS

Each time you are able to type one of these paragraphs, which are getting longer and more difficult to type, without making an error, you have climbed another rung up the ladder of success. I am certain that you are very proud of what you have been able to accomplish and are now looking forward to typing this paragraph perfectly, then the next, and the next, until you are able to type the one-hundred-word paragraph.

90 WORDS

I have taught many students to type ninety or more words a minute without making a single error. Of course, it does require a great deal of discipline--both mental and physical. It is important that you have the capacity for hard work because it will take a great deal of determination on your part to continue to progress from paragraph to paragraph. It will probably be necessary for you to consult with your teacher regularly for typing tips.

Drill 5

In the nucleolus of the nucleus and in the cytoplasm of each cell are mole-
cules of ribose nucleoprotein, which is quite different from the desoxypen-
tose nucleoprotein comprising the genes. The removal of the nucleus from
a cell causes the remaining cytoplasm to very rapidly lose its ribose nucleoprotein, for ribose nucleoprotein of the cytoplasm and the nucleolus is
catalytically formed under the auspices of the genes.

Drill 6

Methyl alcohol, ethyl alcohol, ethylene glycol, and olive oil--and other
highly lipid soluble substances--pass through the cell membrane. These are
enzymes which can phosphorylate glucose. After the glucose is phosphory-
lated, it becomes soluble in the lipoid matrix of the cell membrane. Then
the glucose is dephosphorylated, and the phosphate carrier compound which
has carried the glucose through the membrane diffuses.

Drill 7

Glucose and amino acids cannot pass through the pores of the cell and also
are nonsoluble in lipoid materials. There is a much higher concentration
of some ions in the cellular cytoplasm than in the fluids surrounding the
cells. Usually there is an abundance of potassium, magnesium, and phos-
phates inside the cell. The active transport of various substances to
maintain the intracellular environment permits normal cellular function.

ACCURACY STUDY 27
INTENSIVE CONCENTRATION DRILLS—
REVERSE TYPING

Purpose: To require intensive concentration, thereby facilitating the acquisition of the mental discipline necessary for accurate typing.

Features: These drills are shown typed backwards to compel you to concentrate totally on each letter in each word and will easily be readable when typed correctly.

Line: 75 spaces

Directions: Type each paragraph on a line-for-line basis, reading from right to left, and type each line perfectly two times. Once you make an error in typing a line, begin a new line immediately and type that line until you type it perfectly. In view of the fact that these drills require extreme concentration, you will probably encounter difficulty in typing these drills. Nevertheless, it is imperative that you acquire the mental discipline necessary for accurate typing. You are to type each line BACKWARDS, reading from right to left, and when you complete a line, the typing will be in the normal sequence of reading. Therefore, you will not encounter any difficulty reading what you have typed. Double-space between each drill and each set of two perfect lines. Type slowly and spell each word out—spelling and typing simultaneously.

95 WORDS

There is a definite correlation between what you are able to type speedwise on these one-minute paragraphs and your net speed on a five-minute timed writing. You will see that as you improve your speed on these one-minute paragraphs, so will your speed increase on the five-minute timed writings. Therefore, by developing your speed on these paragraphs, you will simultaneously and rapidly improve your productivity on longer timed writings. Practice these drills every day.

100 WORDS

One of the finest feelings you will ever experience will be the first time you are able to type one hundred words a minute perfectly. I wish I could find adequate words to express the exhilaration you will feel once you are able to type this paragraph in a minute without an error. I know that the first time I typed perfectly at that rate was one of the happiest days of my life. You are close to experiencing this wonderful sensation, and if you are successful, you will be considered an expert typist.

105 WORDS

You have now reached the point in your typing development where you are considered a typing expert. It will become increasingly difficult for you to type each of the succeeding paragraphs, as each is longer than the preceding one, and consequently is more difficult to type. In order to progress, you must decide to work more diligently than you ever did before in order to continue your upward climb in typing proficiency. You will find that what is true in the field of typing is also true in other fields of endeavor.

Drill 1

Many cells of the human body, like unicellular animals such as the amoeba, have the ability to ingest foreign particles by phagocytosis. When a foreign particle touches a phagocytic cell, the touched area immediately invaginates, and the surrounding areas evaginate, to enclose the foreign body in a well, preparatory to ingestion. The normal surface configuration of the cell redevelops after ingestion of the foreign particle.

Drill 2

Unknown are the factors that cause cells to phagocytize foreign particles, but cells have the capability of phagocytizing certain substances easier than others. For instance, electropositive particles are phagocytized more easily than are electronegative particles. Conversely, smooth particles are not as easily phagocytized as rough ones. The inability of macrophages to phagocytize the body's own tissues is understandable.

Drill 3

Fortunately, all the structures of the body are usually electronegatively charged and therefore repel phagocytic cells. Phagocytosis is manifested in the human body especially by the cells of the reticuloendothelial system. This system includes the polymorphonuclear cells of the blood, the wandering macrophages of the tissues, the reticulum cells of the lymphoid glands, and the large lining cells of the circulatory system.

Drill 4

New mitochondria, enzymes, phospholipids, nucleoproteins, large polysaccharides, etc., are all continually synthesized in the cytoplasm. The chemical substrates that are essential to support the metabolic reactions are derived from the nutrients of the extracellular fluids surrounding a cell. Controlling the chemical reactions are the protein enzymes, which are concentrated in especially large quantities in the mitochondria.

110 WORDS

As you press onward for higher speeds, you will find that more and more errors will occur initially. This is due to several reasons. First, you have more words on which you can make errors. Secondly, your fingers have to move at an incredible rate of speed. Also, you are beginning to become more tense because you have to type so many words without making an error. However, if you do not become discouraged and practice these paragraphs diligently, you will notice that your accuracy will improve daily and soon all of your errors will be gone.

115 WORDS

At this point you should be able to type straight copy at the rate of ninety net words a minute on five-minute writings. You should now have excellent finger control and be a very productive typist. Of equal importance, however, is your ability to get along well with others. After all, you must work with others, and in order to achieve success in life, you must be able to work harmoniously with others. To achieve success is why you have worked so diligently on your typing, and you must work just as diligently on developing your personal relations with others.

120 WORDS

You have spent a considerable amount of time and put forth a tremendous effort to reach this level of typing proficiency. I know you are exceedingly proud of your accomplishments, as only a few typists are able to type straight copy at this rate of speed without making an error. I am also proud of you because I know you have paid your dues. It has taken an extraordinary amount of personal dedication and discipline to reach this level of excellence. What you have learned in typing can be applied in all of your endeavors and will produce very gratifying results. It has worked for me.

Drill 5

While this particular assignment is very demanding, you must persevere and, if possible, laugh at your difficulty in typing backwards. Slowly but surely, you will be acquiring better concentration, and as you do, you will find that the number of mental errors you make will decrease until, much to your surprise, you will be making very few concentration errors. The best way for you to eliminate concentration errors is by spelling out each word, typing letter for letter. In typing backwards, you are compelled to spell out each word, as it is the only way you can type this assignment with complete accuracy. It may seem to you to be nonsensical to type backwards, but it will be very beneficial, believe me.

Drill 6

By now, you probably are beginning to acquire the mental discipline you need in order to be able to concentrate completely on your typing--spelling out each word, letter for letter--thereby greatly reducing the number of typing errors you will make on a timed writing. You probably are smiling more as you are beginning to master the art of typing. Your prospects for employment will be greatly enhanced once you develop a high level of skill in typing. You probably no longer dread the thought of having to type. Of even greater importance, you have learned something about yourself--you were able to persevere under the most trying circumstances, and you have now acquired the mental discipline necessary to become a very successful person in typing as well as in other areas.

ACCURACY STUDY 26
INTENSIVE CONCENTRATION DRILLS—
PARAGRAPHS/UNUSUAL WORDS

Purpose: To provide the mental discipline necessary for fast, accurate typing by compelling absolute concentration.

Features: These drills contain a concentration of medical terms. There is a mixture of ordinary and unusual terms. Because of the unique way of typing them, these drills will compel you to concentrate more completely on each typed stroke than ever before.

Line: 75 spaces

Directions: Type each paragraph on a line-for-line basis, and type each line perfectly three times—not necessarily in succession, but in total. Double-space between groups of three perfect lines. You are to type each line BACKWARDS, reading and typing from right to left. Despite the frustrations you may encounter, continue to strive for perfect typing and perfect rhythm. Be sure to check your work carefully.

125 WORDS

I know you are wondering if it is possible for you to make your fingers go fast and accurately enough so you can complete this paragraph in a minute. You know how difficult it has been for you to complete the preceding paragraph. It will be much more difficult to type this one satisfactorily. Therefore, make up your mind that you will have to expend a great deal of energy and that it will require a great deal of determination in order to succeed. You must also be able to relax completely so you will not become too tense. Tenseness is your greatest enemy when speed typing. Therefore, think positive and relax.

130 WORDS

You have reached the last paragraph in these progressive speed drills. You have now reached the championship class among typists and have acquired the digital dexterity that only a few typists have mastered. It will tax all of your energy, determination, tenacity, and positive thinking in order to type this paragraph in a minute without an error. If you are successful, you will have a most satisfying experience, because you will realize that you have joined a select group of typists, those who can type very rapidly and accurately. You are on your way to a level of typing proficiency that will amaze and please others as well as yourself.

Drill 2

It is rather easy to determine if you are making errors due to a lack of concentration. Your error-analysis chart will reveal the fact that you are leaving out letters, adding letters, transposing letters or words, or doubling the wrong letter. Errors of this type clearly indicate a somewhat less than total concentration on what you are typing. In order to type accurately, your concentration must be so absolute that you are completely oblivious to what is going on around you. Also, your concentration must be so thoroughly focused on each word you are typing that you are unable to comprehend what you are typing. You should read the copy for duplication only, not for comprehension.

Drill 3

Whenever students fail to respond to the preceding assignments, it has been generally true that the ultimate solution to the problem is the most dreadful experience of all--typing backwards. This subjects the student to the most extreme mental pressure, and it also subjects the student to the most trying typing exercise imaginable. Initially, many students get very frustrated. Some become very angry and upset because of the difficulty of typing exactly contrary to the conventional method. Nevertheless, if you will just keep on trying to type backwards, no matter how vexing or frustrating it is, sooner or later you will acquire the mental discipline that is necessary to become a very accurate typist.

Drill 4

To type this paragraph backwards--reading each line of copy from right to left--will require absolute, total, and complete concentration. This kind of concentration is essential if you are to become a highly accurate typist. Many students who made numerous errors prior to completing this assignment became very accurate typists shortly after finishing this drill. It seems as though someone had uttered a magical word. Students are simply amazed at their own transformation as they are able to type both rapidly and accurately. Therefore, it is to your advantage to concentrate intently on typing each stroke in each word, because once you acquire the necessary mental discipline, you will become a highly skilled typist.

SECTION 6

ACCURACY STUDIES

Simple-Vocabulary Words	42	Left Hand, Fourth Finger	65
High-Stroke-Intensity Words	43	Right Hand, Fourth Finger	66
Alternate-Hand Words	45	Left-Hand Words	67
Compound- and Multiple-Stroke Words	46	Right-Hand Words	68
Vertical-Stroke Words	47	Punctuation	69
Double-Letter Words	50	Concentration Drills—Similar Words	70
One-Hand Words	51	Concentration Drills—Long Words	73
Alphabetic Words	52	Concentration Drills—Unusual Words	75
Spacing Drill	57	Intensive Concentration Drills—Paragraphs	77
Shifting Drill	58	Intensive Concentration Drills—Paragraphs/	
Left Hand, First Finger	59	Unusual Words	79
Right Hand, First Finger	61	Intensive Concentration Drills—Reverse	
Left Hand, Second Finger	62	Typing	81
Right Hand, Second Finger	63	Concentration Drills—Split Doublets	84
Left Hand, Third Finger	64	Concentration Drills—Paragraphs	85
Right Hand, Third Finger	65		

ACCURACY STUDY 25
INTENSIVE CONCENTRATION DRILLS—PARAGRAPHS

Purpose: To provide the most intensive concentration drill possible, so as to provide the mental discipline essential for accurate typing. These drills will expose you to the most mentally demanding exercises you have ever typed, and if you will conscientiously strive to master each drill, you will be a vastly improved typist.

Features: These drills are comprised of ordinary words; yet because of the unique way of typing them, these drills will compel you to concentrate more completely on each typed stroke than ever before. Each drill contains pertinent information that may be helpful to you. Read all six drills before typing this assignment.

Line: 75 spaces

Directions: Type each paragraph on a line-for-line basis, and type each line perfectly two times— not necessarily in succession, but in total. Double-space between groups of two perfect lines. Despite the frustrations you may encounter, continue to strive for perfect typing and perfect rhythm. You are to type each line BACKWARDS, reading and typing from right to left. This is exactly opposite to the way you would normally type. The first line:

One of the most difficult tasks for most typing students to develop is

typed backwards twice perfectly will look like this:

si poleved ot stneduts gnipyt tsom rof sksat tluciffid tsom eht fo enO
si poleved ot stneduts gnipyt tsom rof sksat tluciffid tsom eht fo enO

Be sure to check your work carefully.

Drill 1

One of the most difficult tasks for most typing students to develop is the mental discipline necessary to become an accurate typist. Due to the fact that most typists have not developed their concentrative capabilities, these students continue to make countless errors and usually are not happy typists. Oddly enough, most students who are experiencing great difficulty in keeping their minds on what they are typing do not know what they must do in order to get the mental discipline they need in order to type more accurately. It has been my experience that the number one problem in typing is the lack of total concentration, and the best way to develop total concentration is by spelling out each word as you type.

ACCURACY STUDY 1
SIMPLE-VOCABULARY WORDS

Purpose: To increase accuracy in typing short words.

Features: These drills contain a concentration of short words.

Line: 60 spaces

Drill Assignment: Use the drill that corresponds in number with the diagnostic test number.

Directions: Type each line perfectly five times—not necessarily in succession, but in total. If you make an error in typing a line, begin a new line immediately. After you have typed the first line perfectly five times, double-space and begin the second line. Double-space between groups of five perfect lines. Begin typing slowly and increase your speed gradually.

Drill 1

```
in to of is to go do on it at so an if he we us as up or be
and men the six aid boy our you out pit now see not but way
can run dog get fox day too two may man one for aid due top
are her she him two put hot big for our ten dad ran won how
```

Drill 2

```
one but yet try who all put sit set own pay out lay say day
more moor will well wail vote vast vest best boat this that
then than them they work come came year hear here boys girl
toys file tile dial pile mile rile sail sale some dome zone
```

Drill 3

```
lone loan time fine find mine mind pine wind wine nine bind
must dust just guts gust rust type fast last cast mast past
make take lake bake rake wake cake sake like bike kite mike
dike pike what when whom call coil hall hail hale here hear
```

Drill 4

```
city near past does fast slow with best true very want work
give have seek fact like folk help jobs much lack fail task
hard each must went need help down whom fine what paid face
lift many wish will days turn mind once with rate feel find
```

Drill 3   G, H, and I

ganglionic gastritis gastrointestinal geniculocalcarine gestation
glomerulonephritis glossopharyngeal glucocorticoids gonadotrophic

hallucinations haustration headaches hemolysis hypertension hypertrophy
hexamethonium histamine hyperglycemic hyperparathydroidism hypotonicity

idiopathic ileocecal ileum immunizations inotropic insulin interstitial
intercavernous interventricular intrapulmonary isotonic juxtaglomerular

Drill 4   K, L, M, N, and O

kathepsin keratin keratoconus ketosis ketosteroids kidney klebsiella
lactation lactogenic leukemia lipoproteins lobotomized luteinization

macrocytes macrophages magenstrasse mediastinitis meningitis metabolical
metarteriole monocytes mononucleosis multimolecular myeloblastic measles

neocerebellum neostigmine nephropathic nephrotic neutrophilia nociceptive
oogenesis ophthalmoscope osmosis ossicular osteoblasts ovaries oxyblepsia

Drill 5   P, R, and S

paleocerebellum palpitation panhypopituitarism paranoia parasympathetic
parathyroid peristalsis phagocytosis phenolsulfonphthalein phonasthenia

regurgitation repolarization resuscitations retinotectal retrotracheal
reticulo endothelial retina respiratory paralysis retinitis pigmentosa

sacrococcygeus salpingitis schistosomiasis scrupulosity seminiferous
sensation silicosis sinus arrhythmia somatotrophic somesthetic spasm

Drill 6   T, U, and V

tachyphylaxis tachypnea tentorium testes tetraethylammonium thalamus
tachyrhythmia thoracic thrombocytopenia thyroglobulin thyrotoxicosis

ulcer ulcerative colitis unipolarity ureteral urethra urobilinogen
urine diurnal urobilinogen urobilins urogastrone uticarial uveitis

vagotomy valvular varicose vasoconstriction vasodilatation vasomotor
vectorcardiogram ventricular paroxysmal tachycardia ventriculography

Drill 5

```
most mast mere deer dear tear hare hard hair well sell fell
feel kill hill till fill peel pare pear pull pool poll than
away your year many good wood hood food mood mode node noll
turn down ship west east rain feet walk soul sole keys sold
```

ACCURACY STUDY 2
HIGH-STROKE-INTENSITY WORDS

Purpose: To increase accuracy in typing long words.

Features: These drills contain a concentration of long words.

Line: 70 spaces

Drill Assignment: For Diagnostic Test 1, use Drills 1 and 6; for Diagnostic Test 2, use Drills 2 and 7; for Diagnostic Test 3, use Drills 3 and 8; for Diagnostic Test 4, use Drills 4 and 9; for Diagnostic Test 5, use Drills 5 and 10.

Directions: Type each line perfectly five times—not necessarily in succession, but in total. Begin a new line immediately when you make an error. Double-space between groups of five perfect lines. Begin typing each line slowly and gradually increase your typing rate as you get familiar with the line of writing.

Drill 1

```
calisthenics disconcerted questionable introspection surreptitious
subordinates compromising precipitated systematizing idiosyncratic
contaminated journalistic inconsistent complementing psychodynamic
hyperkinetic degenerative partitioning transgression therapeutical
```

Drill 2

```
ecumenically undercurrent disruptively retrospective psychotherapy
undercurrent distractions expeditional abnormalities squeamishness
totalitarian professional underdevelop precipitation proselytizing
uproariously pediatrician perseverance recrimination cataclysmical
```

Drill 3

```
eccentricity incarcerated abridgements methodologies paradoxically
convergences malnutrition arithmetical psychological schizophrenic
antithetical unauthorized tractability opportunistic interspersing
predilection unassailable decisiveness compassionate expeditionary
```

ACCURACY STUDY 24
CONCENTRATION DRILLS—UNUSUAL WORDS

Purpose: To provide maximum mental discipline, which is absolutely essential for fast, accurate typing. These drills will compel absolute, total, and complete concentration.

Features: These drills contain a preponderance of scientific and medical terms. This will be one of the most difficult assignments you have typed or will ever type. Yet it is vitally important that you master typing these unusual words, as it will provide you with excellent mental discipline that is essential to good typing. These lines are double-blocked according to each letter of the alphabet.

Line: 75 spaces

Directions: Type each line perfectly two times—not necessarily in succession, but in total. Double-space between groups of two perfect lines. In view of the fact that these scientific and medical words are exceedingly difficult to type, you must type each line very slowly, spell each word out—typing letter for letter—and allow for some frustration as you will probably make a few more errors than usual. Nevertheless, do not get discouraged, continue to strive for good accuracy, and endeavor to type at a slow, rhythmic rate.

Drill 1   A, B, and C

acetylcholine acidophilic acidosis actomyosin adenosine adrenocortical
agglutinogen agranulocytosis albuminoid aleukemic amenorrhea asthmatic

ballistocardiograph basal ganglia basophilic bathesthesia bilirubin
bradycardia bronchitis bronchospirometry bulboventricular beri-beri

carboxymethylcellulose carboxypolypeptidase carcinogenic carcinomatosis
cardiospasm cardiovascular carotenoid cerebrospinal chronaxie cirrhosis

Drill 2   D, E, and F

decarboxylation decibels defibrillation desmosome desoxycorticosterone
deaminase dehydration diabetes diastolic Dibenamine dihydrotachysterol

edema electrocardiography electroencephalogram electrolyte emphysema
encephalography endocrinology endometriosis erythroblastosis fetalis

familial fasciculation fibrillation fibula flatulence flocculonodular
fibrinolysin filariasis flavoproteins fluoroscopic follicular femoral

Drill 4

disseminated increasingly elucidations flexibilities acrimoniously
universality disconnected dictatorship authorization jurisdictions
encyclopedia unofficially optimistical sophisticated certification
peripherally explications artificially investigative resuscitation

Drill 5

cohesiveness interpreting partisanship insensitivity nostalgically
superstition veterinarian disastrously nutritionists healthfulness
recognizance incapacitate continuances revolutionary instinctively
evangelizing effervescent metaphysical intravenously meteorologist

Drill 6

rhapsodizing machinations discomfiture hallucination indefatigable
condominiums persuasively successfully possibilities disseminating
postponement extravaganza interminable preoccupation improprieties
ecstatically monopolistic inflationary automatically vilifications

Drill 7

restaurateur misdemeanors masquerading confrontation intransigence
exorbitantly enshrinement preposterous intentionally unprecedented
entrepreneur embezzlement precariously realistically admissibility
gratuitously abstruseness transcendent manipulations gubernatorial

Drill 8

usuriousness codification annihilating interceptions diametrically
legitimizing mobilization recalcitrant irresponsible fictionalized
complexities deficiencies unquenchable deductibility electrocution
excoriations unregenerate inconsolable immunologists unflinchingly

Drill 9

fulminations loquaciously lexicography parenthetical biorhythmical
excruciating insinuations melodramatic fundamentally protectionism
lasciviously presumptuous editorialize choreographer topographical
sporadically symbolically jeopardizing precipitously spontaneously

Drill 5

continuation controllable disciplining authorization congressional
disregarding disorganized refreshingly decriminalize irresponsible
enthusiastic delineations requirements informational grammatically
appreciative applications acknowledged establishment excessiveness

Drill 6

merchantable minimization impressively magnificently unconsciously
salesmanship tranquillity sophisticate superlatively transcription
recalcitrant perpetrators constructive undergraduate disappearance
compensating appreciation chastisement entertainment reconsidering

Drill 7

cohabitation destinations equalization interrogating technological
distribution transitional commutations progressively realistically
counterpoint kleptomaniac pathetically exceptionally confrontation
civilization perseverance vanquishable comprehension inconceivable

Drill 8

secessionist apprehension insurrection unenforceable abnormalities
constituency miscalculate imponderable personalities automatically
dramatically introduction consultation disproportion sensitivities
unreasonable compartments inauguration investigative compassionate

Drill 9

extrapolated misinterpret expectations transgression unequivocable
affectionate neutralizing encountering contradictory manifestation
unparalleled deficiencies infrequently conveniencing questionnaire
rehabilitate indignations intimidating unfortunately parliamentary

Drill 10

shortcomings irresistible enthusiastic ambassadorial inappropriate
persistently introduction availability unfortunately justification
denomination performances considerably discrepancies vulnerability
differential preferential asphyxiation justification philanthropic

Drill 10

teleprinters sociological budgeteering colonizations anachronistic
visibilities accumulating implications consciousness embarrassment
irreversible enthusiastic ratification bureaucracies collaborative
superstellar abstractions characterize preponderance tantalizingly

ACCURACY STUDY 3
ALTERNATE-HAND WORDS

Purpose: To increase accuracy in typing alternate-hand words.

Features: These drills are comprised of alternate-hand words.

Line: 60 spaces

Drill Assignment: Use the drill that corresponds in number with the diagnostic test number.

Directions: Type each line perfectly five times—not necessarily in succession, but in total. Begin a new line immediately when you make an error. Double-space between groups of five perfect lines.

Drill 1

it rod when with right angle social ancient antique quantity
is the city them sight fight vivify emblems dormant fiendish
of aid than then chaps chant dismal visitor auditor sorority
to and when turn bogus blame mantle proviso visible neighbor

Drill 2

do got girl duty giant handy island prodigy problem ornament
so row wish hand flame right shanty audible enchant clemency
if man roam clan civic forms panels suspend element toxicity
an roe hang dirk their gowns formal rituals augment mementos

Drill 3

am men they rich girls corps ritual figment torment neurotic
by may pale both vigor clams burial socials emblems rigidity
us for busy down ivory tutor disown dispels formals problems
he did name lane world usual airmen disowns rituals provisos

ACCURACY STUDY 23
CONCENTRATION DRILLS—LONG WORDS

Purpose: To enhance accuracy by improving concentration, thereby facilitating the typing of long words.

Features: These drills consist of words containing 12 or 13 strokes each. The sequential arrangement of the words is not in a definite stroking pattern. This will compel total concentration because it is impossible to anticipate the patterns of each word. In other words, there is a mixture of vertical strokes, alternate-hand strokes, and so on.

Line: 66 spaces

Directions: Type three perfect lines of each line—not necessarily in succession, but in total. Double-space between groups of three perfect lines. In view of the fact that you will be typing high-stroke-intensity words, it will be advisable to spell out each word—typing letter for letter. Type all ten drills.

Drill 1

transcendant consequences intellectual investigation congressional
preservation relationship constituents unnecessarily necessitating
astonishment coordination requirements uncertainties accreditation
vicissitudes compromising identifiably proliferation reimbursement

Drill 2

conservative enlightening idiosyncrasy manufacturers determination
strengthened subordinates unacceptable approximately insignificant
indefinitely discriminate presidential opportunities administering
commissioner respectively overwhelming promiscuously inappropriate

Drill 3

professional confirmation distribution irresponsible mismanagement
deficiencies specifically arrangements picturesquely significantly
particularly deliberately conservative disillusioned parliamentary
anticipating accumulation quantitative authorization contradictory

Drill 4

prosecutions remuneration commercially controversies traditionally
ridiculously suppositions insinuations concentration practitioners
intimidation intervention consistently interestingly championships
neighborhood construction orchestrated international demonstration

Drill 4

```
span make dory paid worn torn mend half prod dock ogle pend
mend lend envy odor maid paid laid pair lair hair chap burn
turn curl fury firm lake bush lays idle rosy dish isle risk
halt iris wish fish male form goal dual gory dial hale also
```

Drill 5

```
profit icicle sleigh emblem sicken quench lament clench she
shame quake shake flair tight fight sight tithe eight widow
bigot blend usual digit audit spend amend fiend penal slept
amble bugle endow whale focus title shale cycle chair autos
```

ACCURACY STUDY 4
COMPOUND- AND MULTIPLE-STROKE WORDS

Purpose: To increase accuracy in typing compound- and multiple-stroke words.

Features: These drills are comprised of compound- and multiple-stroke words. A compound stroke is one in which two or more consecutive strokes are made by two or more different fingers of the same hand; for example: *point*, in which the letters *poin* are struck by the fingers of the right hand consecutively. A multiple stroke takes place when two compound strokes involving both hands occur in one word. Example: *most*, which involves two fingers of the right hand, followed by two fingers of the left hand.

Line: 60 spaces

Drill Assignment: For Diagnostic Tests 1 to 4, use the drill that corresponds to the diagnostic test number. For Diagnostic Test 5, use Drills 1 and 4.

Directions: Type each line perfectly five times—not necessarily in succession, but in total. Begin a new line immediately when you make an error. Double-space between groups of five perfect lines.

Drill 1

```
lag hag nag toy coy had ban dam ram now out won win tin bin
dim pit hid has hat hot not let new who two boy hit his mat
nip sin lie tap our can pot put pat say ran van day fan tan
her way new few hat hot ton one tip top pet cap pit set ran
```

Drill 2

```
lies time sail fail wail rail fine cost find bout rout talk
walk what main mean cure pure view pose fair fine find file
vein rein rain sure shop ship take more live this stop mire
most jobs mast past last luck pick post cast mast lost rose
```

Drill 7

complement compliment inert invert invent dairy diary scar scare score
choose chose chosen fonder founder flounder troop troupe change chance
inspiring aspiring toast taste fault flaunt skin skein wrecked wracked
vain vein vine prey pray sell cell sever severe serve grander grandeur

Drill 8

hypothesis hypotheses stain strain word world thesis theses rout route
edition addition audition action auction wine wind intimate intimidate
message massage persecution prosecution banana bandana bonanza sun son
decent descent descend interior exterior inviable inviolable toll told

Drill 9

by buy bye sifting shifting preserve persevere fanatically frantically
imminent eminent nose noose decease decrease million mullion poor pour
professional processional lurch lunch fiend fried friend serial cereal
lung lunge pleading pleasing fete feet feat feast deficient sufficient

Drill 10

hall haul horse hoarse fame flame frame wane wain cause clause eye aye
obvious oblivious residential presidential quit quiet quite dire dirge
bell belle not knot write right cache catch floor flour parcel partial
lighting lightning stair stare pose poise road rode rodeo radio or oar

Drill 11

pose posse possess possession avenge revenge beat beet quarter quartet
assemble ensemble mien mine mind middle meddle muddle contact contract
poll pole cents sense fail flail colon colony sale sail soil tale tail
metal medal defied denied deer dear ail ale picking pickling prickling

Drill 3

knack poise ration endure daily option quite quiet might be
begin piano person there where whether ignore ignite tempts
paint power lower flower tower personality personal persons
that more thing welfare wings confrontation singing ringing

Drill 4

serious combination fundamental institutions advantage were
information pursuits perhaps inspiration financial pictures
influence imagination available achievement everything that
let general vindication around someone conscious stupendous

ACCURACY STUDY 5
VERTICAL-STROKE WORDS

Purpose: To increase accuracy in typing vertical-stroke words.

Features: These drills contain a concentration of vertical-stroke words. A vertical stroke is made when one finger has to strike two or more consecutive keys on different rows of the keyboard. Example: *raze*, in which the letters *az* are struck by the A finger consecutively. Vertical strokes are among the slowest in typing, and a great deal of practice is required to develop fluency in typing them. These drills are arranged so that the first drill concentrates on vertical strokes beginning with the A finger and progresses from left to right to the L finger.

Line: 60 spaces

Drill Assignment: Determine which fingers were involved in making errors. Do drills for all fingers involved.

Directions: Type each line perfectly three times—not necessarily in succession, but in total. Begin a new line immediately when you make an error. Double-space between groups of three perfect lines. Inasmuch as it is difficult to make vertical strokes, begin typing each line very slowly and gradually increase your typing tempo as you become accustomed to the stroking pattern.

Drill 1   A Finger

aquacade aqualungs aquamarines aquaplanes aquarelle aquatint
azaleas azide azimuths azine azo azoic azonal azoth azoturia
jazz dazzle hazard haze razor bazaar jazz dazzle raze razors
buzzard hazard lizard blizzard pizza bazaar buzzard blizzard

Drill 1

an and angle angel be bee bin been bend but butt butte buff bear bare
bore boar beer bier here hear hair hare flair fair fare stakes steaks
concert convert verse averse adverse disperse diverse inverse immerse
rehearse reverse clutch crutch blood flood mug smug snug defray delay

Drill 2

rub tub grub scrub club construct instruct pulse repulse engage enrage
unstrung unsung drunk dunk sunk attach attacks attack fir fur per purr
chasseur chauffeur way weigh decay delay dismay display scratch snatch
canvas canvass draft draught affect effect adopt adapt adept loan lone

Drill 3

hew new knew proceed precede succeed recede dear deer ware wear to too
wait weight wake blue blew birth berth sake shake stake except excerpt
sage stage dodge lodge fog flog back black claque plaque threw through
clack crack alack attack bake brake break fake flake fine find ail ale

Drill 4

ton tone smile simile bough bought brought sought though thought tough
closet closest formally formerly board broad forth fourth later latter
prescribe proscribe breath breathe berth birth coarse course lane lain
deserts desserts peace piece access excess their there weather whether

Drill 5

corporation cooperation advise advice might night knight plains planes
savage salvage trough through threw thru principal principle seam seem
see sea seen scene great grate create crate site cite sight fake flake
sweater sweeter grandma grammar aid aide pair pear pare powers powders

Drill 6

stationary stationery cede seed preceding proceeding formally formerly
led lead minute minuet ingenuous ingenious addition edition loose lose
council counsel consul continual continuous dying dyeing devise device
farther further father envelop envelope capital capitol sleigh sleight

Drill 2 S Finger

swat swear sweet sword sweep swell swift sway swap swastikas
swamp sweat swallow swindle swing swollen swizzle swim swing
blows flows lows laws blows saws views flaws paws news brews
glows aglows slows sews sows grows brows bows tows cows rows

Drill 3 D Finger

ceded cedar cecum ceiling celebrate celebrity celery censure
deeded decedent deceased deceit decelerate deceive deception
eccentric ecclesiastic ecology eclipses economy ecstasy echo
educate education educe editor editorial edition edify edict

Drill 4 F Finger

friend from frame fruit fragrance fragment fragile fractures
craft raft draft swift lift rift drift left soft shaft often
break brake braggart braggadocio bravo bramble brass brought
bring brassiere brave brawl bread breach breast broil bruise

Drill 5 F Finger

grab grabble grace gracious gradate graduate graft graduates
ground great gray gruesome greed gregarious grievance gritty
grip grippe grist grizzle groom grocery growling groin gross
groove ground growth growling grove grotesque grotto grudges

Drill 6 J Finger

jump jumpy just justly jumble jumper junction juncture junky
jungle junior junk juniper junket junta junto jurat justices
injure injury injurious injuriousness injunction injudicious
injustice inject injector injectable injudiciousness injects

Drill 7 J Finger

hub huddle hues hued huff huffy hug huckster huge humorously
human humanism humanity humanize humble humid humor humorous
hyaline hyalite hybrid hydrant hydraulic hydrogen hydroplane
hypnotic hymn hymnal hypnosis hypnotism hyphen hypercritical

Drill 3 Quotation Marks, Periods, and Commas

He said, "I am glad that you won the lottery," and I replied,
"What are you going to do with all of the money that you just
won?" He said, "I am going to put a lot of the money in U.S.
savings bonds--for my old-age protection--and I am also going
to visit New York City, Boston, Philadelphia, Chicago, Miami,
and Washington, D.C. I have desired to visit those places at
least once, and it appears, I am going to be able to do it at
long last. I shall have fun. I shall learn much. It may be
worth all of the expenses involved. Why don't you come too?"

Drill 4 Dashes and Hyphens

He works on a day-to-day basis. I endeavored to send a form
for out-of-town employment to a major self-help organization
which is well-developed organizationally. A self-help group
is an indispensable resource for the community and motivates
many fair-to-middling individuals to aspire to creatively do
something--no matter how small--to contribute to the welfare
and well-being of our fine country. Under the circumstances
it is our well-intentioned privilege to do our utmost to get
a better understanding--for whatever it is worth--of what we
can do in this respect. We are certain to do our very best.

ACCURACY STUDY 22
CONCENTRATION DRILLS—SIMILAR WORDS

Purpose: To improve accuracy by developing absolute and complete concentration on each word to be typed.

Features: These drills contain a concentration of similar-looking or similar-sounding words, thereby compelling intense concentration.

Line: 70 spaces

Directions: Type each line perfectly three times—not necessarily in succession, but in total. Double-space between groups of three perfect lines. In view of the fact that concentration plays a major role in accuracy—more students make more concentration errors than any other type of error—it will be necessary for you to *spell out each letter of each word.* It may cause you to reduce your typing speed initially; however, once you become accustomed to typing on a single-stroke-recognition basis, your typing speed will return to your normal rate and the number of errors you make will be reduced dramatically. Therefore, type *letter for letter.* Type each drill.

Drill 8   J Finger

much mucilage muciferous muck mucus mud muddy muffler muffin
tumble jumble mumble stumble rumble fumble humble jumble rum
myoglobin myrrh myself mystery mystic mystify mythologically
myopia mycology myasthenia musty musket music mustard museum

Drill 9   J Finger

numeration nuncupative nuptial numerology numerous numerator
nuance nub nuclear nucleus nudge nullify nuisance number nut
nylons any many anyway anytime anything synonymous gymnasium
nun numb nuncle numerical numismatic numismatically nummular

Drill 10   J Finger

umbel umbilicate umbilicus umbrage umbrageous umbrella umbra
immunologist immune tumultuously inhumanity autumnal jumpers
unabated unabridged unaccustomed unavailable uncouth uncruel
unhurried unused unusually unutterable unyielding unnumbered

Drill 11   K Finger

kibitz kibitzer kick kickers kidnap kidnapper kidney killers
killer kilogram kingdom kilt kimono kind kindle kindred king
kitchen kite kitty kitchenette kinescope kinematics kilogram
kindergarten kin kindred kill kinetic kiss kidskin kingcraft

Drill 12   L Finger

load loaf loan lobby lobsters lockers locomotive logarithmic
logic logistic lonesome long longevity longitude loopy lowly
color follow hollow folders oleander soliloquy oleomargarine
hold fold told cold sold bold gold old stole whole hole mole

ACCURACY STUDY 21
PUNCTUATION

Purpose: To improve accuracy in typing punctuation marks.

Features: These drills contain a concentration of various punctuation marks. Each drill emphasizes two or more punctuation marks, and this emphasis is clearly indicated in each drill.

Line: 65 spaces

Directions: Type three perfect copies of each line—not necessarily in succession, but in total, of each punctuation drill on which you made too many errors in the Pretest. You are to double-space between the groups of perfect lines. Begin typing each line slowly, and gradually increase your typing rate until you are typing as fast as you can with accuracy.

Drill 1   Commas and Periods

The girls saw birds, dogs, cats, sheep, cows, bulls, goats, chickens, roosters, ducks, turkeys, rabbits, and a goose on my brother's farm. They, it seems to me, were surprised to see a variety of crops growing: corn, potatoes, beans, tomatoes, lettuce, cucumbers, cantaloupes, watermelons, kale, celery, spinach, cabbage, collard greens, and squash. This was quite an educational experience for them. It was helpful and something they would be able to tell their friends.

Drill 2   Question Marks, Periods, and Exclamation Points

Who is it? It is I. What do you want? I want to talk to you. What about? Open the door and find out. Why should I? It is important! How can I know that it is important? Well, you know me and I would not say it if it was not so! All right, then, I will open the door. I am glad that you did. Why? You won first prize in the raffle drawing that the state conducted last night. First prize, as you know, is a trip around the world traveling first class on one of the best airplanes anywhere. It's worth opening the door!

ACCURACY STUDY 6
DOUBLE-LETTER WORDS

Purpose: To enhance accuracy in typing double-letter words.

Features: These drills contain many words possessing double letters. Double-letter strokes are among the slowest strokes in typing. The drills are arranged in alphabetic sequence.

Line: 61 spaces

Drill Assignment: For Diagnostic Tests 1 to 4, use the drill that corresponds to the diagnostic test number. For Diagnostic Test 5, use Drills 1 and 4.

Directions: Type each line perfectly five times—not necessarily in succession, but in total. Begin a new line immediately upon making an error. Double-space between groups of five perfect lines. In view of the fact that these drills are arranged alphabetically, it will be advisable for you to type all four drills, if you have problems making double-letter strokes, in order to acquire fluency in making any type of double-letter combination.

Drill 1   A, B, C, and D

aardvark aardwolf Aaron Aaronic bazaar aardvark Aaron bazaars
bubble ebb rabbit bobbing robber hobby gobble bobbing bubbles
succeed occasion account accompany accrue occurs successfully
add middle forbidden adduce fiddler addition adding forbidden

Drill 2   E, F, G, and L

feel heel steel bleed engineer three sweet breeze beef degree
effect coffee differ difficult off affluent efforts officials
bragging dagger luggage baggage suggest struggling braggingly
dollar ball all bull rally allege parallel hall all fill well

Drill 3   M, N, O, and P

recommend summary communicate comment programmers commitments
planner running winning skinny dinner planned connect sinners
too boom book coordinate broom cool brook zoom look root boot
appear supply opportunity wrapped suppress appraise appraised

Drill 4   R, S, T, and Z

horror embarrassment worry error corruption current embarrass
class pressure assume assail grass assassination essence pass
pretty attention ghetto attrition attack attract utter better
jazz buzzard puzzles dazzle embezzlement blizzards embezzling

Drill 4 W, X, and Z

waterer watering watcher wasps warrantable weave waltz whiz warble wafter
axe axiomatic extreme exceed exalt exception extra expeditious exorbitant
zinnia zinc zonally zealous zeroes zany zealot zigzag zigzagging zoophyte

ACCURACY STUDY 20
RIGHT-HAND WORDS

Purpose: To enhance accuracy in typing by developing much better control of all the fingers of the right hand.

Features: These drills reflect a systematic approach in perfecting reaches involving the fingers of the right hand. There is a concentration of difficult words in each line, so as you develop fluency in typing them, you will note a corresponding improvement in your accuracy and finger dexterity.

Line: 75 spaces

Directions: Type each line perfectly five times—not necessarily in succession, but in total. Double-space after typing five perfect lines. Begin typing very slowly, and gradually increase your typing rate until you are typing at your fastest accurate rate. Type all three drills.

Drill 1 H, I, J, and K

hippopotamus hokum haphazard humor hilum hilly homonym humanize homonyms
initiate inimitable injustice ionic iniquity injurious idiosyncrasy inky
jeopardize jerkily junk jumpy jujitsu junction jolly jalousie jalopy jut
kimono knowledge kilometer knuckles kick kind khaki kayak kamikaze kills

Drill 2 L, M, N, and O

lackadaisically luminescent limited lumpy lolly lazily loyalty loop loin
magnanimity monopoly minimum maximum minikin monotonous murmurous murmur
numinous nihility numbs nylon nozzle napalm number nominee nihilism nook
optimum oilily olympians ominous olympic opinions opposition opportunity

Drill 3 P, U, and Y

poliomyelitis pump pumpkin puny portrait population points physical puppy
ultimatum usual unusual union upon uphold unruly unscrupulous unambiguous
yolk yipper yellowy youth yourselves yokel yacht yardage young yesteryear

ACCURACY STUDY 7
ONE-HAND WORDS

Purpose: To increase accuracy in typing one-hand words.

Features: These drills are comprised of one-hand words so that fluency can be developed in typing them. One-hand words are very difficult to type and are typed at a slower rate of speed than most other words. These drills are arranged alphabetically to facilitate locating particular letter combinations for corrective drilling.

Line: 60 spaces

Drill Assignment: For Diagnostic Tests 1 to 4, use the drill that corresponds to the diagnostic test number. For Diagnostic Test 5, use Drills 5 and 6. These directions only apply when doing corrective practice for Chart 3.

Directions: Type each line perfectly three times—not necessarily in succession, but in total. Begin a new line immediately upon making an error. Double-space between groups of three lines. In view of the fact that these drills are arranged alphabetically, it may be advisable for you to type all six drills—if you have problems typing one-hand words—in order to acquire fluency in typing one-hand words. Otherwise, if you can identify a particular type of one-hand word that gives you difficulty, you can concentrate on that particular corrective drill. For example, one-hand words on the right side of the keyboard may be causing you a great deal of difficulty. In that eventuality, you will practice only those words in which the letters are located on the right side of the keyboard.

Drill 1   A, B, C, and D

```
abate abstracter affected acts are agree aware axe avert as
battered badgered bar base bees beware better beg bear best
cabaret cabbage cage cad cease cedar crab craft cast caters
dab dad daze dare debt deeded debase decade drab draw dress
```

Drill 2   E, F, G, and H

```
eager ease east ebb edge eggs ersatz ewe eve evade exceeded
facade fade far fear federate fewer fever fat fracas feeder
gadget gaffer gage gate gas gaze gear geese geezer greatest
hill hilly him hilum hip hippy hokum holly holy hilly hippy
```

Drill 3   I, J, K, and L

```
ill ilium ilk imply ink ionium ion inky ill ink imply ilium
jink jolly jump junk jumpy junky join joy junky jolly jumpy
kill kiln kimono kin kink kip kill kiln kimono kin kink kip
lily limp loin loll lolly look loop loom loon lull lip look
```

ACCURACY STUDY 19
LEFT-HAND WORDS

Purpose: To enhance accuracy in typing by developing much better control of all the fingers of the left hand.

Features: These drills constitute a systematic approach in mastering reaches involving the fingers of the left hand. Many of the words contained in these drills are difficult to type. As you develop fluency in typing them, you will notice a marked improvement in your finger dexterity and accuracy.

Line: 75 spaces

Directions: Type each line perfectly five times—not necessarily in succession, but in total. Double-space between groups of five perfect lines. In view of the fact that each line contains a concentration of difficult words, it will be advisable for you to begin each line slowly, gradually increasing your typing rate on each subsequent line until you have reached your fastest accurate typing rate. You are to type all four drills.

Drill 1   A, B, C, and D

abstracter achievable acquisitive analyzable attributable azaleas attest

battered badgered baggages beatable bibliography believably benedictions

combining cabaret cabbages ceded cubic criminologists created categorize

decedent desegregate deeded dazzled dissatisfied dependence debate dazed

Drill 2   E, F, G, and Q

exacerbate extravaganza eczema erasable exceeded exactly equate excerpts

fabric fragrance freeze freezer federate fragmentation fateful frustrate

galaxy gaze gigantic garage garbage grazes greatest gregarious gravitate

quarrels quarry quantity quackery quench quandary quagmire quadruplicate

Drill 3   R, S, T, and V

recede reverberate reveille regrettable rebellion rebate reaction regret

staggered squatters segregated sextet swerved sewage seesaw sequence sew

tumultuous terrestrial twist tweezer traverse tranquility tattoo tatters

visualize vex vast vertex vertigo vertebra vegetables vegetate venerable

Drill 4 M, N, O, and P

minimum milk milium mink minikin monopoly mummy mull milium
nip nylon noon nook null nun nylon ninny null no nylon nook
oil oilily onion only opinion oil oilily onion only opinion
pin pip plunk polo polio pulp pull pumpkin puppy pony pulpy

Drill 5 R, S, T, and V

raze raft ragged rare rate react recede rebate reverberates
saw savage saber seaweed stab scarf seesaw starve segregate
tattered tax tract teeter terse trace tweezer tweezers text
vacate vat veer vegetate vested verse vertebra vex vertexes

Drill 6 W, X, Y, and Z

wade wader wafer waft wafter wag ward war ware was wear wet
weave web weft west wrest wart wasted waterers watered wave
union you extra extracted sextet union you extra exaggerate
zebra zest zed zagged zebra zest zag zagged zebra zag zebra

ACCURACY STUDY 8
ALPHABETIC WORDS

Purpose: To enhance accuracy in typing by developing fluency in typing various letters of the alphabet.

Features: These drills consist of a systematic approach in mastering a variety of strokes involving the entire alphabet and including the more difficult reaches on which most errors are made.

Line: 60 spaces

Drill Assignment: Determine which fingers were involved in making errors. Do drills for all fingers involved.

Directions: If you are typing corrective drills on one or several letters of the alphabet, you will type five perfect lines of each line—not necessarily in succession, but in total. Begin a new line immediately upon making an error. If you are to review the entire keyboard, you will type three perfect lines of the first two lines of each drill. If additional drills are necessary, you will type three perfect lines of the final two lines of each drill.

Drill 1 A Stroke

abstracts abstractions abash abroad ability affects affected
are argue arguments agree agreement art arts artist artistry
avert averted avoidance avalanche avail availed availability
axone axiom axis axle axenic axial aqua aquarist aquiculture

Drill 1   Q Stroke

quadrennial quadrennium quadrilateral quadrille quench quest
quadrumvirate quadruped quadruple quadruplets quadruplicates
qualifier qualm quality quantal quantifiable quantifications
quantity quarter quarantine quarantinable quarrel queasiness

Drill 2   A Stroke

a at attack attribute attributable attire attach attachments
act acts actions accompany acquires acquisition acquisitions
as ash ashamed ashore ascend ascension ascribe astonishments
awake awaken aware awareness awesome azaleas azimuth azurite

Drill 3   Z Stroke

zip zipped zipping zippers zippy zircons zirconate zirconium
zirconic zithers zizith zodiac zombi zonal zonate zone zones
zoo zoomorphic zoogenic zoogeography zoological zoology zoom
zoophyte zonally zounds zygote zeppelins zymotic zygomorphic

ACCURACY STUDY 18
RIGHT HAND, FOURTH FINGER

Purpose: To improve accuracy in typing by developing better control of the fourth finger of the right hand.

Features: This drill emphasizes a systematic approach in mastering reaches involving the fourth finger. The words selected for this drill concentrate on letters which are struck by the fourth finger as well as specific reaches on which many students make errors.

Line: 60 spaces

Directions: Type each line perfectly three times—not necessarily in succession, but in total. Double-space between groups of three perfect lines. Begin typing each line slowly, and gradually increase your typing speed.

Drill 1   P Stroke

package pacific painstaking papaya pajamas pageants papillon
phase pharmacy pheasant phonics pharmacist phenomenal pauses
piano pianist piazza pin pimple pica picador picadors pickle
points poinsettia poisons poisonous pole polemics population

Drill 2   B Stroke

batter battered badge badgered barren basin basket basketful
brown brought bring break breakfast brook brooks brand brain
be bees beat believe beware bewail between bewitch begin bet
basic basify base baseballs barrel barren bazooka barometers

Drill 3   C Stroke

cab cabaret cabbage cabin cabinet cable cache cactus captain
cease ceaseless cedar cede ceded ceil ceiling cell celebrate
crop crops crack cracker cradle craft crafty cram cramp cave
center central centric ceremony centipede certain cerebellum

Drill 4   D Stroke

dance dandruff danger dangle daze dazzled dazzling dare darn
deacon debt dead deed deeded debacle debase debate debit dew
decade decadent decedent decided deception decry desegregate
drab draft drag dragging draw dragnet dragon dragoon drained

Drill 5   E Stroke

ebb ebony ebullience excelled excellent excellence eccentric
ecclesiastic ecclesiastical echelon eczema eclaire ecologist
ego egocentric egoism equip equal equator equally equivalent
evacuate evade evaporate evasive eve even event evolve extra

Drill 6   F Stroke

fable fabric facade face facet facetious fade fabulous fancy
fear fearless feast feature federate felicity few fewer fend
fracas fraction fragile fragmentary fragmentation fragrances
fatal fatalistic fat fate fathom fateful fault fatuous favor

Drill 7   G Stroke

gab gabble gable gag gage gad gadfly gadget gaff gaffer gate
gear geese geest great generic gelatinize gelatinous general
gig giggle gigantic genius gift gilt ginger girl giraffe get
graduate grain grand graze granite great greatest gregarious

ACCURACY STUDY 16
RIGHT HAND, THIRD FINGER

Purpose: To enhance accuracy in typing by developing better control of the third finger of the right hand.

Features: These drills constitute a systematic approach in mastering reaches involving the third finger. The words that have been selected not only contain a number of letters involving the third finger but, equally important, stress particular reaches on which many students make errors.

Line: 60 spaces

Directions: Type each line perfectly three times—not necessarily in succession, but in total. Double-space between groups of three perfect lines. Begin typing each line slowly, and gradually increase your typing speed.

Drill 1   O Stroke

oak obedience object oblivion occurrence occupy odors odious

onus onyx ooze oozy opal open opened opening operational out

operate operable ophite opiate opinion opinionated opportune

oppress oppression oppressive optimal optimism optimum optic

Drill 2   L Stroke

label labor lap laborious labyrinth lapidary laconic lacquer

lazy lazily lament laxative lexicon layette lead leaf ledger

limp library lying liege lien like lilies limited limitation

lubricant lucid lucidity ludicrous lug luggage lullaby lulls

ACCURACY STUDY 17
LEFT HAND, FOURTH FINGER

Purpose: To improve accuracy in typing by developing better control of the fourth finger of the left hand.

Features: These drills reflect a systematic approach in perfecting reaches involving the fourth finger. The words contained in these drills not only include a number of letters involving the fourth finger but, in addition, emphasize specific reaches on which many students make errors.

Line: 60 spaces

Directions: Type each line perfectly three times—not necessarily in succession, but in total. Double-space after typing three perfect lines. Start typing each line slowly, and gradually increase your typing tempo.

Drill 8   H Stroke

hiatus hibernate high hill hilly him hilum hinder historical
holiday holly holy home homely homonym homeroom homicide hop
human humane humor humility humanity humanize humbug humdrum
hydrants hybrid hydrogen hydrology hygiene hymn hypertension

Drill 9   I Stroke

iodic idiot iodine iodous ionic ionium ionize ionosphere ion
imbricate imbroglio imitable imitate implication immediately
indefatigability indefensibility individual input inimitable
iniquity initiate initiation initiative injurious injustices

Drill 10   J Stroke

jib jibe jiffy jig jigger jigsaw jitney jingle jink jive job
joist joke jokes joker journal jolly jolt josh jostle jovial
jugular juice juicer juicy jujitsu julep jumble jumpy jumper
junction juncture jungle junk jurisdiction juror justify joy

Drill 11   K Stroke

khaki khan kick kicker kid kidnap kidney kiss kowtow kernels
kill killer kiln kilocycle kilogram kilometer kimono killers
kind kindle kindly kindness kinescope kinetic kinetics knots
knead kneel knell knick knife knight know knowledge knuckles

Drill 12   L Stroke

liable liability liaison libel liberate limit liberation lie
load loaf loan lobby lobe lobster local locale location lock
loin loll lolly long look loop loom lower loon lowly loyalty
luminescent lump lunar lunatic lung lunge luster lurk lazily

Drill 13   M Stroke

maximum minimum milk mill militia militate military mind may
minnow minikin minimal minimize mink minister ministering my
mollify mollusk moment momentum monetize monk money monopoly
mummy mull mumps multiplicity mullion murmur murmurous money

Drill 3   E and I Strokes

counterfeit retrieve protein hierarchy caffeine anxiety heir

spontaneity lien leisure believe kaleidoscopic alien freight

achieve deceit relieve foreign reprieve forfeited brief rein

heinous science surveillance friend reimburse relief receive

ACCURACY STUDY 15
LEFT HAND, THIRD FINGER

Purpose: To enhance accuracy in typing by developing better control of the third finger of the left hand.

Features: These drills emphasize a systematic approach in perfecting reaches involving the third finger. The words selected for these drills concentrate on letters which are struck by the third finger as well as basic reaches on which many students make errors.

Line: 60 spaces

Directions: Type each line perfectly three times—not necessarily in succession, but in total. Double-space between groups of three perfect lines. Start typing each line slowly, and gradually increase your typing tempo.

Drill 1   W Stroke

wade wader wafer waft wafter wag wagging wagon wage waif was

waist waive walk ward war ware wasp warrantable washer watch

web weevil weft weeping welfare wench west wet western weeps

wrest wrench wrestle wriggle wrinkle wrist writ writing whiz

Drill 2   S Stroke

saber sabbatical sacrifice sag sagacity safety sanctimonious

scalp scallop scarce scarf scavenger scintillate scissor sew

squabble squad squalor square squash squat squatters squawks

steeve steer stencil sterilize stitches stimulate stipulates

Drill 3   X Stroke

extreme exceed exaction exceeding exceedingly exalt excepted

exception exceptional excise external externally externalize

excerpt exonerate exorbitant exorcism exoteric explicit exit

extra extreme extrication expedite expeditious expel expiate

Drill 14   N Stroke

numbs ninety nickel niece nibble nineteen nimble need needed noise noisy nobility nocuous nomenclature nozzle nominations nuance nuclear nucleus nudge null nullify numbers numerously numinous nurture nuptial nursery nurse nylon night neighbors

Drill 15   O Stroke

oil oilily oiliness okra old oleomargarine olive olympic odd oleographs olympiads ominously omelets ominous omnibus omega omnificent omnipresent omnivorous once oneness onerous onion opportunity oppose opposable opponent opposition opposite on

Drill 16   P Stroke

physical physician physics physicist physiology physiography pious piously pioneer pink pinnacle pip piping plunk plunger polish police polo poll pole polemics public publicity puppy pull pulmonary pulley pulpit pump pumpkin puny poliomyelitis

Drill 17   Q Stroke

quack quackery quad quadrangle quadrant quintet quinine quit quaff quaffer quagmire quail quaint quake quale quick quaver quality qualified qualification qualify qualitative quandary quarrelsome query quarry quart quench quest quests questions

Drill 18   R Stroke

rabbi rabbit rabid rarity raccoon race racial racism rackets racketeers radio radiator raffle raft rag ragged range razor rebellion recap recast recede receded receipt receipts reply revamp reveille reveal reverberate reverberant reverberation

Drill 19   S Stroke

seclude secret secretary seaweed sedge seesaw seize seizures segregate sewage sextet sextuple sequence sequential squalid staff stage stagger staples stapler starchy state statements swag swagger swallow swampy swerve switch swell sweets swift

Drill 2   D Stroke

dab dabble dad daffodil daffy dainty daiquiri daily dangling

debonair debrief debris debutante debt debenture debate deal

drawn drawer dread dreary dream dredge dribble dress dresser

divide dividend divisive dock docket doctrine divulge doctor

Drill 3   C Stroke

credit creatures creative creation credible credence cranial

cube cubes cubic cubicles cuckoo cucumber cart carts carried

chain chair chaise chafe chalk chalet charter champion catch

cast castle casket category cashew cater catalog coax coaxed

ACCURACY STUDY 14
RIGHT HAND, SECOND FINGER

Purpose: To improve accuracy in typing by developing better control of the second finger of the right hand.

Features: These drills consist of a systematic approach in mastering reaches involving the second finger. The words contained in these drills not only include a number of letters involving the second finger but also emphasize specific reaches on which many students make errors.

Line: 60 spaces

Directions: Type each line perfectly three times—not necessarily in succession, but in total. Double-space after typing three perfect lines. Begin each line slowly, and gradually increase your typing rate.

Drill 1   I Stroke

ilex ill ilium illegal illegitimate illness illustrative ilk

image imagery imaginable imbalance imitates iniquities imbue

ink inmate innate inning innocence innuendo inquisition inky

irresistibility irrigate irritable irritant itemization itch

Drill 2   K Stroke

kaddish kaiser kayak kale kaleidoscope kamikaze kangaroo key

keel keen keep keeper keeping kennel kernel kerosene kettles

king kingdom kingly kink kinsfolk kip kismet kiss kisses kit

kitchen kite kitten kleptomaniac knack knap knave knee known

Drill 20   T Stroke

tatters tattered tattoos tattooer tawdry taverns taut taught
teach teachable technical technique technology teeter temper
trace tract trade traction tradition tragic tragedy transact
twist twister twitcher twinkle twirl twinge tweezer tweezers

Drill 21   U Stroke

ulcerous ulcerated ulterior ultimate ultimacy ultimatum unit
umbilicate umbilicus umbrage umbra umbrella umbrellas umpire
unconscious unconquerable unluckily unmanly unscrupulous use
upswing upstate uptake uranium upwards usable usage umpirage

Drill 22   V Stroke

vacate vacation vacuum vagabondage vagarious vagrant various
vagueness valve values valvular vampire vampirism vanquished
veal veer vegetable vegetate vehicles veiling velvety velvet
verse vest versus vertebra vertebras vertex vertexes vertigo

Drill 23   W Stroke

waste water waterer waterfall watt wave wax wavy waxy waiver
wear weak week wet wearily weapon weary weather weave weaver
wrangle wrap wrapped wrath wreak wrought wreathe wreck wrens
watch watchers watchful whack whacking whacky wrack wretched

Drill 24   X Stroke

xanthate xanthene xanthic xanthone xenias xerarch xylophones
xenophobo xenophobia xerography xylography xylem xylan axles
axe axes axile axiom axiomatic axis axle axenic axial auxins
auxiliary box boxes boxer boxy buxom exact exactly extremely

Drill 25   Y Stroke

yacht yachting yak yam yank yap yard yardage yawl yaws yield
yielding yip yipping yodel yodels yogurt yoke yokel yolk you
yore yonder your yourself young younger yoga youngster youth
yourselves youthful yowl yucca yule yurt yachts yipper yolks

Drill 5   H Stroke

habit hack haggle harper hamper handle handicap haunt hanger

hinge hint hip hippopotamus history historicize hither hitch

hoard hoarse hoary hoatzin hoax hokum hobble hoise hoist hit

hurt hunt hunger hump hurdle humpy hunter hurl humiliate hip

Drill 6   N Stroke

names naive naked napalm narcissism narratives nation narrow

never nebulous neutrons nemesis necessary neurotic nefarious

nice nicety niche nigh night nihilism nihility nip nipple no

noble nocturn nocturnal nominal nominee nod nook noon noodle

ACCURACY STUDY 13
LEFT HAND, SECOND FINGER

Purpose: To increase accuracy in typing by developing better control of the second finger of the left hand.

Features: These drills constitute a systematic approach in perfecting reaches involving the second finger. Great care has been taken in selecting words that not only involve a number of letters which are struck by the second finger but, in addition, reinforce specific reaches on which many students make errors.

Line: 60 spaces

Directions: Type each line perfectly three times—not necessarily in succession, but in total. Double-space between groups of three perfect lines. Start each line slowly, and gradually increase your typing tempo on succeeding lines.

Drill 1   E Stroke

eager ear eagle earl easy early easement earth earn ease eat

edema edge edginess edible edict edification education edify

era erase erasable errors eradicable erupt erratic eradicate

exact exaction exceed exalt extreme except exception extinct

Drill 26   Z Stroke

zabaglione zaffer zamia zanders zanily zaniness zany zagging

zeal zealot zealous zebra zebu zenith zenithal zeolite zooms

zephyr zero zeroes zest zesty zigs zigged zigging zigzagging

zigzag zigzagged zinc zincate zincite zinnia zinnias zoology

ACCURACY STUDY 9
SPACING DRILL

Purpose: To improve accuracy in spacing between words and punctuation marks.

Features: These drills are comprised of exercises in which it will be necessary to space after left- or right-hand strokes. Some of the drills require spacing after left-hand strokes, while others require spacing after right-hand strokes, and still other drills are a combination of the two. To facilitate identifying each type, each drill is labeled so that you can work on your particular spacing problem.

Line: 60 spaces

Drill Assignment: Determine whether you made more spacing errors after left- or right-hand strokes. Then do the appropriate drills. For example: If most spacing errors were made after right-hand strokes, do Drill 1 or 4. If too many spacing errors were made after both left- and right-hand strokes, do Drill 3. *Always use your right thumb in spacing! Never use your left thumb.*

Directions: If you are having difficulty in spacing after either left- or right-hand strokes, type ten perfect lines of the type that is giving you problems. On the other hand, if you are having problems spacing after both left- and right-hand strokes, type five perfect lines of each drill. The five perfect lines do not have to be consecutive.

Drill 1   Right Hand

; l k j h j k l ; l k j h j k l ; l k j h j k l ; l k j h j

p ; / o l . i k , u j m y h n u j m i k , o l . p ; / o l .

y h n u j m i k , o l . p ; / o l . i k , u j m y h n u j m

j u y h n m j u y h n m j u y h n m j u y h n m j u y h n m

Drill 2   Left Hand

a s d f g f d s a s d f g f d s a s d f g f d s a s d f g f

d s a s d f g f d s a s d f g f d s a s d f g f d s a s d f

q a z w s x e d c r f v t g b r f v e d c w s x q a z w s x

e d c r f v t g b r f v e d c w s x q a z w s x e d c r f v

ACCURACY STUDY 12
RIGHT HAND, FIRST FINGER

Purpose: To improve accuracy in typing by developing better control of the forefinger of the right hand.

Features: These drills comprise a systematic approach in mastering reaches involving the index finger. The words that have been selected not only contain a number of letters involving the forefinger but, equally important, reinforce specific reaches on which many students make errors.

Line: 60 spaces

Directions: Type each line perfectly three times—not necessarily in succession, but in total. Double-space between groups of three perfect lines. Begin each line slowly, and gradually increase your typing rate.

Drill 1   U Stroke

unaffected unaccustomed unadulterated unaware unbeaten ultra
unruly unruliness unquiet unquestioning unprecedented upsets
upon uphold upholster upholstery upkeep upper upright unions
unscientific unsheathe unsophisticated unusual unsought used

Drill 2   J Stroke

jab jack jacket jade jaded jaguar jalousie jalopy jazzy jams
jealous jealousy jeer jell jelly jeopardy jeopardize jerkily
jinx jitter jobber jockey jocose jocular jogs joiner joiners
journey jubilee judges judgment judicial juggle juggler jugs

Drill 3   M Stroke

machine machinery mad madam magazine magnanimous magnanimity
milium mimic milo mimicry mincing minimal minimization minus
mines minuet minute mock mobilize modify mogul moll mortgage
monolithic monotony monotonous monument monumental momentary

Drill 4   Y Stroke

yes yean years yearling yearn yeast yells yellow yelp yeasty
yerk yesterday yesteryear yet yew yelper yearly yearning yap
yamen yammer yarrow yare yauld yaw yawn yawning yellowy yews
yellowish yachting yardarms yauld yaupon yolked yolky yokels

Drill 3 Left and Right Hands

```
a b c d e f g h i j k l m n o p q r s t u v w x y z a b c d
e f g h i j k l m n o p q r s t u v w x y z a b c d e f g h
a ; q p s l w o d k e i f j r u g h t y f j r u d k e i s l
a ; z / s l x . d k c , f j v m g h b n f j v m d k c , s l
```

Drill 4 Right Hand

```
him dim pin kin no, to, do, so, pay say day may top mop pop
hymn pain lain rain main many body lady puny pony only baby
party hardy today sorry tardy dimly stick money honey carry
then them they pull hull dull maul doll hill bill will sill
```

Drill 5 Left Hand

```
act are bar bat sat ace was saw see sea tax few dew due far
here hear wear tear tact raze rear text bear bare faze fade
thing their there those where whose looks books beats beets
cares cease trace tract costs waste waxed seize right tight
```

ACCURACY STUDY 10
SHIFTING DRILL

Purpose: To improve accuracy in making capital letters.

Features: These drills contain a concentration of capital letters, which compel frequent shifting. Drills 3 and 4 are arranged so that the lines with the least number of capital letters are at the top of each drill, while those that contain the greatest number of capital letters are located at the bottom of each drill.

Line: 60 spaces

Drill Assignment: For Diagnostic Tests 1 to 4, use the drill that corresponds to the diagnostic test number. For Diagnostic Test 5, use Drills 3 and 4. These directions only apply when doing corrective practice for Chart 3.

Directions: Type three perfect lines of each line—not necessarily in succession, but in total. Begin typing each line slowly, and gradually increase your rate of speed until you are typing at your fastest accurate typing rate. This is a very difficult and tedious drill; yet you must master this phase of typing in order to acquire a good typing skill. Therefore, be prepared for frustrations, and persevere. Type all four drills to correct faulty shifting. Make certain that the shift key is completely depressed when you strike the letter to be capitalized.

Drill 1   R Stroke

rare rarefied rafts rascal rascally raze rasp raspberry rate
reach react reaction read reader rebate realize rebuke rebel
reciprocate reciprocity reflex reflexive regrets regrettable
resolute resolution respect retail retaliate restitute recur

Drill 2   F Stroke

fictitious fickle field figure figuration finances financial
frame frangible fray frazzle frank frankfurter freeze frozen
flux fly flurry fluffy foliage foil focal focalize foist fox
fed fender fencing festival fecund feed feeder fencer fervor

Drill 3   V Stroke

vellum vein venerable ventriloquist venture verb verbal very
vivid vivify vivisection vixen vizard vivacious vitiligo vat
visual visualize vision virulence virtue village villa vapid
valedictorian valiant valuate variate various variegated vex

Drill 4   T Stroke

tarp tarpaulin tar tarnish tape tapestry talk talking tactic
terminate terminal terrace terrestrial territory territorial
transaction transcend travel tranquil tranquility transcribe
transfer transferred traverse travesty tree treasurer treaty

Drill 5   G Stroke

gain gainful galaxy gaze gauge galley gang gangsters garnish
generation generic genesis genteel geography geomagnetic gem
glacial glad gladiator glare glaze glebe globe glorious glow
gaffer goggle gong gorgeous graft grass grade grab greed gas

Drill 6   B Stroke

bit bitter big bigger bike bikini bile bilingual bilk bilker
boy born borrow borough burrow boss book books blossom bloom
buffet buffer bug bugaboo bugle budget budgetary bag baggage
beatable beauty beautiful best bestiary bestow bezel bezique

Drill 1

```
aA ;: qQ pP sS lL wW oO dD kK eE iI fF jJ rR uU gG hH tT yY
aA ;: zZ /? sS lL xX .. dD kK cC ,, fF jJ vV mM gG hH bB nN
aA bB cC dD eE fF gG hH iI jJ kK lL mM nN oO pP qQ rR sS tT
uU vV wW xX yY zZ uU vV wW kK xX zZ mM aA nN bB mM cC oO gG
```

Drill 2   (Shift for each letter; do not use the shift lock.)

```
A : S L D K F J G H F J D K S L A : S L D K F J G H F J D K
S L A : S L D K F J G H F J D K S L A : S L D K F J G H F J
A : Q P A : Z ? S L W O S L X . D K E I D K C , F J R U F J
V M G H T Y G H B N F J R U F J V M D K E I D K C , S L W O
```

Drill 3

```
The Shifting For Capital Letters Is Very Tedious To Master.
Try To Spend Some Time Working On Your Major Problem Areas.
Typing Will Be Fun If You Go About It The Championship Way.
It Will Be A Great Skill If You Learn How To Shift Rapidly.
```

Drill 4

```
Much Skill Is Required To Learn How To Type Satisfactorily.
Mary Must Develop Perfect Timing In Order To Make Capitals.
It Is Not Easy Learning How To Type Rapidly And Accurately.
If You Want To Type Well, You Will Master This Phase Of It.
```

ACCURACY STUDY 11
LEFT HAND, FIRST FINGER

Purpose: To enhance accuracy in typing by developing better control of the index finger of the left hand.

Features: These drills consist of a systematic approach to mastering reaches involving the index finger. The words that have been selected not only contain a number of letters involving the forefinger but also reinforce specific, basic reaches on which many students make errors.

Line: 60 spaces

Directions: Type each line perfectly three times—not necessarily in succession, but in total. Double-space between groups of three perfect lines. Begin each line slowly, and gradually increase your typing tempo.